Creating Dynamic Schools Through Mentoring, Coaching, and Collaboration

JUDY F. CARR, NANCY HERMAN, AND DOUGLAS E. HARRIS

Association for Supervision and Curriculum Development
Alexandria, Virginia USA

Association for Supervision and Curriculum Development
1703 N. Beauregard St. • Alexandria, VA 22311-1714 USA
Phone: 800-933-2723 or 703-578-9600 • Fax: 703-575-5400
Web site: www.ascd.org • E-mail: member@ascd.org
Author guidelines: www.ascd.org/write

Gene R. Carter, *Executive Director;* Nancy Modrak, *Director of Publishing;* Julie Houtz, *Director of Book Editing & Production;* Darcie Russell, *Project Manager;* Shelley Kirby, *Senior Graphic Designer;* Barton Matheson Willse & Worthington, *Typesetter;* Dina Seamon, *Production Specialist*

All Web links in this book are correct as of the publication date below but may have become inactive or otherwise modified since that time. If you notice a deactivated or changed link, please e-mail books@ascd.org with the words "Link Update" in the subject line. In your message, please specify the Web link, the book title, and the page number on which the link appears.

PAPERBACK ISBN-13: 978-1-4166-0296-5 • ASCD product #103021 • s11/05
PAPERBACK ISBN-10: 1-4166-0296-8
e-book editions: retail PDF ISBN-13: 978-1-4166-0353-5; retail PDF ISBN-10: 1-4166-0353-0 • netLibrary ISBN-13: 978-1-4166-0351-1; netLibrary ISBN-10: 1-4166-0351-4 • ebrary ISBN-13: 978-1-4166-0352-8; ebrary ISBN-10: 1-4166-0352-2

Quantity discounts for the paperback edition only: 10–49 copies, 10%; 50+ copies, 15%; for 500 or more copies, call 800-933-2723, ext. 5634, or 703-575-5634. For desk copies: MEMBER@ascd.org.

Library of Congress Cataloging-in-Publication Data

Carr, Judy F.
   Creating dynamic schools through mentoring, coaching, and collaboration / Judy F. Carr, Nancy Herman, and Douglas E. Harris.
       p.   cm.
   Includes bibliographical references and index.
   ISBN 1-4166-0296-8 (alk. paper)
   1. School supervision.   2. Mentoring in education.   3. Group work in education.
I. Herman, Nancy, 1950– .   II. Harris, Douglas E.   III. Title.

   LB2806.4.C37 2005
   371.2′03—dc22   2005021083

12 11 10 09 08 07 06 05   12 11 10 9 8 7 6 5 4 3 2 1

CREATING DYNAMIC SCHOOLS THROUGH

MENTORING, COACHING, AND COLLABORATION

List of Figures

ACKNOWLEDGMENTS

OUR OWN JOURNEYS HAVE BEEN RICH WITH OPPORTUNITIES TO COLLABO-rate throughout our careers with colleagues in schools and districts, colleges and universities, foundations, professional organizations, and state departments of education.

We are grateful to Zelda Zeleski and teachers and administrators in the Chittenden South Supervisory Union in Vermont who saw the value of districtwide training for mentoring and colleague support. They inspired us to begin this project. We thank former superintendent Kenneth Eastwood and the six teachers on assignment in the Oswego City School District in New York—Julie Burger, Cathleen Chamberlain, Irene Dewey, Marie Smith, Dianna Tice, and the late Sandra Harrison—for sharing their Shoulder to Shoulder mentoring program and modeling the essence of high-quality collaborations while designing and implementing professional development. We appreciate, as well, the support, questions, encouragement, and ideas we have received from Vermont administrators and teachers in the Franklin Central Supervisory Union, Franklin Northeast Supervisory Union, Franklin Northwest Supervisory Union, Grand Isle Supervisory Union, Lamoille South Supervisory Union, St. Johnsbury School District, and Washington Central Supervisory Union; and also from administrators and teachers in Somers, Connecticut; and Columbia, South Carolina. Teachers and administrators in the Manatee and Sarasota County

School Districts in Florida have been most generous in sharing their experiences and materials from the excellent mentor training, colleague support, and leadership initiatives taking place in their schools and districts.

We learned much about ways to support development of extended learning communities focused on improved student learning from deputy commissioners Herman "Bud" Meyers and Douglas Walker of the Vermont Department of Education and from Edith Beatty, Fern Tavalin, and Susan Boyer of the Teacher Quality Enhancement Project at the Vermont Institutes. We also wish to thank the curriculum coordinators in the Vermont Standards and Assessment Consortium who provided us with opportunities to present at their conferences and receive critique on early versions of this work.

Laurey Striker, Peter French, and Janice Fauske of the University of South Florida, Sarasota/Manatee, have provided valuable support for the completion of this book.

Finally, the contribution of our editors Joyce McLeod and Darcie Russell to the fine-tuning of the manuscript has been an ongoing, rewarding experience that has markedly improved the final product. And to Scott Willis and all the folks at ASCD who do so much to support collaborative efforts at all levels of the educational system, we express our deepest gratitude.

1

BUILDING PROFESSIONAL RELATIONSHIPS

MENTORING, COACHING, AND COLLABORATION ARE SHARED PROCESSES, A shared journey of commitment to effective practice and improved learning for all students. In a learning community, adults and children alike are learners as they experiment, give and receive feedback, and use and offer support. When these interactions are embedded in the school culture, a new synergy evolves and a shift occurs—a shift to the forward momentum of collaborative school renewal.

In many states, recent legislation calls for mentoring new teachers to improve their teaching and to help keep them from dropping out of the profession. In response, mentoring programs have sprung up and many schools and districts are working earnestly to implement them. Too often, though, this work is seen as being about "them" (the mentees) rather than about "us" (educators as a group). At the simplest level, this narrow view means that participants see mentoring as a one-way street in which the mentor supplies the new teacher with support and information but receives nothing in return. In more complex terms, experienced teachers lose valuable opportunities to exercise mentoring skills and to support one another in a quest for continuing growth.

Imagine a scenario in which all professional educators in a school are themselves learners. Work is done in partnership with colleagues in pairs, in small groups, and in collaboration with the whole faculty. The focus of this work is ongoing engagement in a process of purposeful inquiry

1

designed to improve student learning. This scenario is not yet typical, but it is entirely possible. Pockets of collaboration exist in almost all schools, and the value of expanding them in size and scope cannot be overstated.

PURPOSES AND SKILLS

Mentoring, coaching, and collaboration are types of colleague support that encompass a set of overlapping knowledge and skills relevant to all players in the educational enterprise. Figure 1.1 distinguishes among the various types of colleague support and lists purposes, typical participants, and content and skills pertinent to each type.

The relationships described in Figure 1.1 are never entirely discrete, but clarifying the roles and purposes of the formal relationships helps to define the knowledge and skills necessary to support a fully collaborative environment. Although some people come by these concepts and processes quite naturally, being clear about roles and purposes and making a commitment to learn and to implement these practices together is the heart of a truly shared journey. Use the information in the figure to plan professional training that supports mentoring, coaching, and collaboration. Figure 1.1 is also a guide for the design of templates and materials that can be used as tools throughout the process of school renewal. It is the framework we used to develop the chapters in this book.

Relationships

Mentoring, coaching, and collaboration are not ultimately about programs, tools, or schedules. Rather, the essence of each is the relationships built around shared purposes and mutual goals among the adults involved. Unlike personal relationships that center on the extent to which the parties *like* one another, professional relationships in schools and districts require understanding of diverse styles, knowledge of effective approaches to communication and dialogue, awareness of critical aspects and stages of team relationships, and the ability to deal with issues in ways that will effectively sustain the relationship.

Personal Styles

Many of the conflicts that arise between people in schools have to do with differences in individual styles of reflecting, interacting, and problem

FIGURE 1.1
Knowledge and Skills for Mentoring, Coaching, and Collaboration

Professional Relationship		Purpose	Participants	Skills
Mentoring		Retention Induction Support	Experienced professionals working with colleagues new to the profession or new to the school	Conferencing Assessing needs Observing and giving feedback Receiving critique Planning for change Critiquing Providing advocacy Enhancing management skills Dealing with logistics Planning curriculum, instruction, and assessment
Coaching	Peer Coaching	Instructional improvement Professionalism	Matches or pairs the following participants: Experienced professionals with experienced professionals; Experienced professionals with new professionals; New professionals with new professionals	All the above skills and the following: Improving instruction and assessment Teaching demonstration lessons Benchmarking Using description vs. judgment when giving feedback Addressing individual issues
Collaboration	Study Groups	Professional growth Organizational change	Administrator with new professionals Experienced professionals with experienced professionals Experienced professionals with new professionals	All the above skills and the following: Using protocols to guide collaborative inquiry

(figure continues on next page)

FIGURE 1.1 (continued)				
Professional Relationship		Purpose	Participants	Skills
Collaboration (continued)	Committees	Policy decisions Curriculum development Action planning	Experienced professionals with experienced professionals	All the above skills and the following: Developing meeting process skills, confrontation skills, and skills for dealing with difficult people
	Departments and Teams	Planning instruction Curriculum planning Assessment	Experienced professionals with new professionals	
	Advisory Councils and Leadership Groups	Governance Issues Recommendations Professional development	Experienced professionals	

solving. Failure to recognize these very natural differences and failure to capitalize on the strengths these differences connote lead to missed opportunities for the educators involved, their students, and the school as a whole. It is useful for those who work in schools to share a common language about styles, to understand what varying profiles mean for interactions, and to know how to work with colleagues who have similar and different styles from their own. Understanding similarities and differences in styles helps to create ways of connecting and builds bridges to understanding. A difference in style does not mean that people cannot work together; often it is the lack of understanding about how a person with a different style sees the world that leads to conflict.

Many inventories are available for the purpose of understanding styles. The Martin Operating Styles Inventory (Martin & Martin, 1989) shows how individuals of particular styles typically operate, not only under normal conditions, but also how they operate under stress. See Figure 1.2 for more information.

Colleagues should use a common styles inventory or a similar framework as a basis for understanding how they can best interact, discussing

FIGURE 1.2
Operating Styles Characteristics

Primary Style	Normal Conditions	Making Decisions	Communicating Information	Nonverbal Cues	Under Pressure
Thinker Gathers data through the left brain channel	Logical Analytical Systematic Organized Fact oriented Deliberate Orderly Rational	Gathers factual data Follows logical, analytical process Makes deliberate choices based on specific criteria Resists being hurried Values making the correct choice	Presents historical background Relies on logical factual information Uses a calm unemotional delivery Written communication is structured, thorough, and contains supporting information in the form of lists, charts, and figures	Has a serious facial expression Dresses neatly and conservatively Briefcase contains business files, supporting documents, calculator, and calendar neatly arranged Values beginning on time and remaining on schedule	Overly serious Emotions hidden Indecisive Inflexible Broods Over-controls Withdraws Judgmental Perfectionist
Feeler Picks up feelings through emotional antenna	Emotional Focuses on feelings People-oriented Friendly Warm Charming Loyal Sensitive to others' needs	Assesses feelings of self and others Determines how alternatives affect others Asks opinion of key people Decides based on most harmonious effect	Creates an informal friendly climate Mixes social dialogue with business discussion Introduces humor to release tension Uses informal notes to personalize written communication	Facial expression accurately reflects emotional mood Dresses informally according to mood, wearing favorite sentimental items Briefcase contains essential business items as well as personal items such as photographs and food Time schedule less important than meaningful interactions	Over-personalizes Blames Vindictive Moody Volatile Impulsive Manipulative Sustains conflict Gossips

(figure continues on next page)

FIGURE 1.2 (continued)					
Primary Style	Normal Conditions	Making Decisions	Communicating Information	Nonverbal Cues	Under Pressure
Sensor Senses small stimuli in immediate environment	Active Results-oriented Confident Competitive Here-and-now oriented Does several things at once Candid Assertive Realistic	Acknowledges the problem Conducts brief, rapid investigation of facts Assigns high priority to problem Begins action immediately Concerned with immediate results	Confronts issues directly, concisely, with candor Speaks with confidence Uses real, concrete examples Writing characterized by brief memos	Physically assertive and dominant Dresses appropriate to task, ranging from casual to formal Briefcase stuffed with office files, magazines, and hobby information Impatient with schedules that hamper "do it now" philosophy	Brusque Short-sighted Combative Hyperactive Distrustful Inconsiderate Compulsive Impatient
Intuitor Gains insight through the subconscious right brain	Creative Imaginative Inner vision Conceptual Asks "why" questions Innovative Idealistic Intellectually tenacious Independent Psychic potential	Asks questions to obtain a complete picture of the problem Brainstorms alternatives automatically Weighs alternatives based on long-range effects Arrives at solution through inner vision	Speaks in global conceptual terms Explains concept using a wide variety of examples Uses analogies to create mental pictures Creates interest through the use of visual images in written correspondence	Sits on the fringe of group activity Dresses in interesting or unusual attire Briefcase contains unusual items representing diverse interests, files of unfinished work, and leading-edge literature Time schedules are ignored when involved in a new interest	Aloof Removed from reality Lack of completion Ignores conflict Impractical Dogmatic Overlooks detail Overly optimistic

From Martin, H. H. and Martin, C. J. (1989). Martin Operating Styles Inventory. San Diego, CA: Organization Improvement Systems. Http://www.ois-martin.com. Used with permission.

and acknowledging these preferences, and planning how to deal with issues that result from their differences. Inventories that identify styles can be found in books or online. The opportunity for team members, department members, and mentor-mentee pairs, for example, to look at their styles, acknowledge how they best interact, and plan how they will deal with differences that emerge in their relationships can forestall communication problems. In the groups we've worked with, these conversations often begin with nervous laughter but soon turn to earnest sharing, discussion, and commitments to future interactions.

DEALING WITH ISSUES

The reality of conflict and difficult people surfaces in nearly every group. Conflict is not something most educators savor; therefore, most are enthusiastic about learning communication strategies for working through (not avoiding) conflict and dealing with difficult people. The most creative and effective solutions often emerge from conflicts that are brought into the open. Once group members understand this basic truth, they value the role of conflict in group interactions.

Some groups or teams find it difficult to gel because of underlying problems. If the problems are caught early enough, the relationship may be revived. Relationships within a group often become unsatisfactory when

• A clear purpose and reasonable goals for the whole group are not articulated.

• Meeting times are not kept or are unrealistic.

• Long-held resentments sabotage the relationship.

• The personalities of colleagues do not complement each other.

• Insufficient attention is given to the relationship—the rationale for partnering people is lacking.

• The expectations of the individual group members are significantly different.

Sometimes we ask educators to write a detailed description of the most difficult collegial interaction they have ever had. These real-world scenarios allow group members to identify common themes across the situations they describe and to practice problem-solving strategies around conflict. We tell them not to identify the person, but to write in enough detail so that the issue is clear. We ask them to include a description of the behaviors that were difficult to work with related to the interaction. In response, one teacher gave the following description:

> We spent months coordinating an interdisciplinary unit among
> 5 teachers. As we began final preparations for our culminating event,
> which had been agreed upon months earlier, one team member began
> to insist that it would never work and we couldn't do it the way we
> planned. This person would not accept that we understood the con-
> cerns, but didn't agree with him. The person walked away and refused
> to participate.

Making Shared Decisions

The principal is no longer the lone leader in the school. Lead teachers, parents, and community members often play critical roles in making decisions that support improved student performance. Within schools, groups involved in decision making may include

Departments. In high schools, teachers who teach the same subject areas often work collectively to plan curriculum, share assessments, and develop schedules.

Teams. Middle school organization is usually team based. Teams are often made of two to five teachers who share a group of students, plan together, and communicate with parents and with colleagues on other teams in the school.

Committees. Many tasks in schools are done by committees, representative groups working together in either short-term or long-term commitments to revise curriculum, plan professional development, select exemplars of high-quality student work, and choose textbooks.

Governance Councils. Representatives of various subgroups (e.g., departments or teams) within the school meet regularly with the principal to make decisions that affect the life of the school community as a whole. In some schools, representative parents or community members are also part of the school's governance council.

See Figure 1.3 for an overview of shared decision making in schools—a process involving individuals and groups in the achievement of group goals related to improved student learning, enhanced programs and practices, and increased resources to support learning.

FIGURE 1.3
Overview of Shared Decision Making

Shared decision making is a **process** of
- interaction;
- assessment;
- communication; and
- problem solving;

involving people with **individual**
- personalities;
- group-work histories;
- conflict styles;
- strengths and weaknesses; and
- interests and needs;

in the development of **shared**
- purposes; and
- processes;

for the achievement of **group**
- cohesiveness; and
- goals

related to improved student learning, enhanced programs and practices, and increased resources to support learning.

TOOLS AND STRATEGIES TO SUPPORT THE GROUP DECISION-MAKING PROCESS

Discussions about team development naturally lead to conversations about decision-making groups that were not productive or were difficult to work in. Many groups work without implementing simple strategies that could help them to avoid conflict and achieve productivity. Decision-making groups can work together efficiently and effectively by setting ground rules, establishing clear agendas, and keeping action minutes.

Setting Ground Rules. Ground rules are agreed-upon norms by which the group operates. They are principles that guide the ways in which group

> ### FIGURE 1.4
> #### Draft of Ground Rules
>
> 1. All meetings will begin and end on time.
>
> 2. To promote efficiency, we will prepare for meetings.
>
> 3. A 10-minute break will be taken every hour-and-a-half during lengthy committee meetings.
>
> 4. Side conversations should not occur during meetings, except as appropriate for small-group discussion of agenda items.
>
> 5. The level of trust will be such that statements and differences expressed within meetings will not be carried beyond the walls of our meeting room.
>
> 6. When a difference of opinion exists about a particular issue, every effort will be made to reach a decision by consensus. (Consensus means all members are willing to live with the decision.) When consensus cannot be reached in what is deemed by the meeting facilitator to be a reasonable amount of time, the decision will be made by a two-thirds majority vote of those present at the meeting.
>
> 7. All group members will support the final product.
>
> _____
>
> From Carr & Harris (1993). Adapted with permission.

members do their work together. Identifying and agreeing to ground rules at the outset establishes an efficient approach to getting the job done and creates a safe working environment in which differences of opinion can be resolved. A group, working independently, can brainstorm, refine, and adopt ground rules. Many groups start with a draft list of ground rules, such as those shown in Figure 1.4, and work to revise and adapt them to best suit the group.

Once the ground rules are adopted, the facilitator and the group should use them consistently; the group should occasionally assess its use of them. The ground rules may be revised whenever the group as a whole decides to do so.

Creating Agendas. An agenda sets the focus of the meeting, helps to ensure that what needs to get done gets done, and establishes the pace that keeps participants engaged. The agenda identifies the topics to be discussed, the time allocated to each topic, and the person who will facilitate the discussion of each item. Sharing information should be handled through memos or a handout provided at the end of the meeting, leaving the space on the agenda for substantive items related to the group's overarching task—items that require the engagement and action of the group to move forward. Meeting topics can be solicited from group members, taken from suggestions in previous action minutes, or generated by the meeting facilitator based on information received or new requirements of the group since the previous meeting. Often it works well to generate tasks for the next meeting at the end of the previous meeting.

Many groups make the mistake of putting too many items on the agenda for the amount of time available for the meeting. Less is more when it comes to setting agendas, and it is best to have no more than two to three items on the agenda for a one-hour meeting, with a maximum of an additional item per hour for longer meetings.

Each item on the agenda should be allocated an amount of time. If the topic is not completed within that time frame, the group should stop and formally decide whether to devote more time (and, therefore, decide from which other agenda item to take the time away) or whether to add the item to a future agenda for continuation.

It is best to list items on an agenda using verbs and describing the task to be completed. Therefore, "Create language arts philosophy statement" is preferable to "Language arts philosophy." A descriptive, active agenda provides a clearer direction and a greater sense of accomplishment at the end of the meeting.

Over time, in combination with meeting minutes, meeting agendas provide a record of the work of the group. Agendas include the name of the group, the date and time of the meeting, and a list of the people invited and included. If attendees are expected to read, do work prior to the meeting, or bring items with them, it is appropriate to add that information to the agenda. The heart of the agenda is the list of items to be completed, the time frame for each, and the name of the persons charged to facilitate the discussions, using the group's ground rules. Figure 1.5 provides an agenda template.

FIGURE 1.5

Agenda Template

Agenda
Day/Date/Time
Department, Team, Committee Name

Read or Do Ahead of Time: _____

Bring to Meeting: _____

Topic: _____ Facilitator: _____ Time: _____

Of course, the most important part of having an agenda is following it during the meeting.

Keeping Action Minutes. Action minutes are a record of the decisions made at the meeting, not a running record of all issues raised or all comments made during the meeting. A template, such as that shown in Figure 1.6, can be used to record action minutes during the meeting. The minutes can then be duplicated at the end of the meeting for members. Action minutes preclude the need for formal typing and presentation of the minutes, which is often a reason that minutes don't get distributed.

We recommend keeping one copy of the action minutes in a notebook that all members can access. That way, stakeholders who miss the meeting can be prepared for the next meeting.

Roles and Responsibilities. Shared decision making requires people to take on the same kinds of roles and responsibilities that we ask students to assume when we teach them to work in effective cooperative groups—a facilitator, a recorder of the action minutes, and a timekeeper.

For some groups, the facilitator is determined by job description, such as when the principal facilitates the governance council or the department chair leads meetings. Other groups assign a facilitator for a given period of time, such as a school year, or rotate the role of facilitator among the members. If you use rotation, we suggest shifting the responsibility only after several meetings, not with every meeting, to allow some continuity of approach.

FIGURE 1.6

Action Minutes Template

Group Name: _____   Meeting Date and Time: _____

Members Present: _____

Members Absent: _____

Decisions Made and Next Steps	Persons Responsible	Time Frame

Possible Topics for Future Agendas: Date and Time of Next Meeting:

The recorder uses the action minutes template to record decisions made during the meeting, including the names of persons responsible for work to be done prior to the next meeting and agenda items for future meetings. At the end of the meeting, the recorder makes copies of the form for the attendees, absent invitees, the notebook, and any others the group wishes to inform.

The timekeeper assists the facilitator by monitoring the group's use of time in relation to the time allocated on the agenda. Often the timekeeper will let the group know when just five minutes are left for a particular task and will guide the discussion if the group needs to decide whether to allow more time for the task to be completed.

GROUP GOALS AND COHESIVENESS

Shared decision making often has been ineffective because the focus has not been on the aspects of schooling most likely to improve student learning— curriculum, assessment, instruction (Fullan, 2001; Mohr & Dichter, n.d.).

Collaboration alone may improve the climate of the school, but it is not sufficient to improve student learning in significant ways. Teachers who are involved in making schoolwide decisions directly related to student learning are more likely to restructure their own classrooms in ways that will improve learning and teaching.

It is essential for decision-making groups in schools to be clear about their purpose and goals. Sometimes these are established outside the group, such as when a school board charges a committee with a task. But in teams that work together over time, the goals of working together often become murky. For example, middle school teams often devolve into groups that spend most of their planning time dealing with discipline issues that concern only a few students. In fact, by the third session focusing on the same students, it is unlikely that much will be accomplished without bringing in outside resources (e.g., the guidance counselor) or gathering new information (e.g., a full-scale evaluation). A new sense of purpose and accomplishment emerges when middle school teams commit to spending three of their five days on issues that pertain to curriculum, instruction, and assessment, leaving just two days for individual student issues or meetings with special educators.

High school departments frequently make the mistake of meeting to deal with administrative matters that could be more effectively dealt with in a memo. When these sessions are used instead to design end-of-course assessments, create learner-focused course descriptions, or share successful approaches to teaching, the culture of the department can change radically, in positive ways.

Stages of Group Development

All decision-making groups—teams, departments, committees, and governance councils—go through predictable stages of development. Tuckman (1965) identified four stages of team development that are still applicable to professional educators in understanding the nature of their work in groups. These stages are forming, storming, norming, and performing. To these four stages, Johnson and Johnson (1994) later added a fifth stage—adjourning.

• **Forming** is coming together as a group, getting to know one another, settling into the group's identity, and having each member embrace his own role in, and importance to, the group.

- **Storming** is the conflict stage, in which differences in styles and goals emerge.
- **Norming** is the stage in which a group works out its own set of expectations about how the group will operate.
- **Performing** is the state in which the group gets the job done; the group moves forward on its work together, whether the work is a short-term process (e.g., a study group conducting an action research project) or a long-term process (e.g., a school governance council overseeing implementation of a school's strategic plan).
- **Adjourning** occurs at the point when the task is completed, when members of the group leave, or when new groups are formed for new tasks focused on improving student learning.

Often when we work with groups in schools, we ask all members to write down a description of a team or committee they have worked with and to state whether the team was productive. Most people easily remember and summarize an ineffective team experience.

When reflecting on personal experiences, teachers are able to see the naturally occurring cycles of group development. They are able to identify the elements that make a team successful or unsuccessful and to brainstorm possible strategies that might have redirected the team in positive ways.

These stages are common in new groups of any kind, and they also recur when mature groups with lots of experience working together encounter new problems, issues, or tasks. The stages are not purely linear; rather, aspects of one stage often continue to appear as the next stage emerges. Awareness of these stages and knowledge about what to do about them can help departments, teams, committees, and governance councils to accomplish the tasks most necessary for improvement of student learning. Leadership to support this work is the focus of Chapter 5.

SHARED JOURNEY

The focus areas and professional relationship suggestions presented in this chapter are central to building the professional relationships that are essential to working toward the goal of improved student learning. This shared journey involves all professional members of the school community in ongoing, collaborative relationships for the purposes of continuous learning and mutual support. In Chapter 2, you will find a framework and interactive approaches for developing and implementing an effective mentoring program that helps to induct, retain, and support new teachers on their journeys to becoming exemplary teachers.

2

MENTORING
NEW TEACHERS

IN CONTRAST TO A STANDARD PROFESSIONAL DEVELOPMENT MODEL THAT is directed at staff at all experience levels, mentoring programs enable and encourage novice teachers to grow and change as they create their own questions and find their own answers in a supportive environment. A mentor working through a structured mentoring program can guide new teachers with strategies that will explore their questions and answers in a timely fashion. Given mentor support, new teachers are more likely to successfully move through the challenging first year of teaching; research shows that mentor programs have positive effects on teacher retention (Huling-Austin & Murphy, 1987; Odell & Ferraro, 1992).

Ideally, mentoring is at least a one-year process and is even better when the relationship lasts for two or three years. In this book, we use the structure of a single academic year, although preparing to be a mentor can easily extend beyond that time frame.

Getting a mentoring program started involves providing potential mentors with professional development to address the what (content), the when (timing), and the how (communication) of mentoring support. A mentoring program requires thoughtful planning and help with professional development to ensure that the relationship between mentor and mentee is productive and ultimately leads to enhanced student learning and job satisfaction for both teachers.

The tools and strategies explained in this chapter are for mentors, new teachers, and administrators who support mentoring programs. We'll explain key concepts related to establishing successful mentoring relationships, as well as provide pragmatic tools and templates for support throughout the year. The material supports independent study, school and district induction programs, and workshops.

GETTING STARTED

When veteran teachers are asked why they want to be mentors, their answers are myriad:

- I want to support new teachers.
- I've been assigned to be a mentor.
- We must have a mentoring program in place by October—it's been mandated.
- We are losing too many novice teachers.
- I want to revitalize my practice.

When teachers make connections with their own first mentoring experiences in order to better understand the mentoring role, common ground is built among the differences in motivation voiced above. When teachers are asked, "Who has mentored you?" and "What was most important to you in how they mentored you?" their responses are also quite varied. One teacher reflected:

> I remember a quiet teacher in my first school who would put gifts on my desk. One time she gave me the outline and all the resources for a geometry unit, another time it was Chiclets—those funny little square pieces of gum. She did this throughout the year. She was a lifesaver (I think that she even put some of those treats on my desk during the year, too). I did not have many materials for teaching mathematics in my class that first year, so the resources she gave me really saved me. I will never forget her kindness and compassion.

Another teacher reflected, "There was a teacher who not only showed me the ropes of classroom management, but she had the greatest sense of humor and kept me in stitches quite often—instead of tears. Having a sense of humor was so important to me, and it still is."

When teachers begin to explore the qualities that make a good mentor by revisiting their own experiences as novice teachers, they easily craft the characteristics of effective mentors that reflect the facts found in the research. By using what they know about positive mentors in their own lives, teachers begin to lay the groundwork for understanding the necessary attributes of a mentor. According to DeBolt (1989, p. 19; adapted with permission), here are the most important characteristics of effective mentors:

- Trustworthy
- Tactful
- Flexible
- Consistent
- Informal
- Willing to share information
- Demanding
- Willing to engage in active, open learning
- Able to listen
- Facilitators
- Respectful
- Committed to providing time to be with the new teacher

Mentors need to draw on their experiences and images of when they were successfully mentored, but they must also move beyond this personal construct to grasp the whole of the mentor and mentee relationship. There is so much mentors can learn about their own practice from their relationship with a new teacher. Invite mentors to be open to learning from the novice teacher. Ask mentors to reflect on a time they worked with or mentored another teacher. What benefits did they receive?

We've often heard mentor teachers say, "I learned so much that it changed the way I teach." Working with a novice teacher was a blessing for this veteran teacher who wrote, "I really didn't have a handle on creating rubrics. This new, right out-of-college teacher taught me how to create them. I feel like I'm staying current."

Considerations When Beginning a Mentoring Program

Now that you know the qualities you're looking for in veteran teachers, you'll need to provide them with the knowledge, tools, and strategies for working with new teachers and a thoughtful plan for implementing the mentoring program.

Selection of Mentors

Crafting a selection process for mentors and clarifying the mentors' roles and responsibilities prior to selection makes teachers and administrators aware of the importance of this job. Mentors are not assigned to be buddies simply for "how's it going" chats. In addition, a mentor provides a mentee more than a checklist of important information, such as policies and procedures. We recommend the following criteria for selecting mentors:

- Candidates should be respected by colleagues for their knowledge and expertise as teachers.
- Candidates should have a strong interest in learning.
- Candidates should have a history of working respectfully and supportively with colleagues.

To encourage the strongest candidates to be mentors, it is critical to offer appropriate incentives. Those incentives may be a creative mix that works for your school or district. Schools often choose rewards such as release time for meetings, stipends, or professional development credits.

Creating Policies and Procedures for a Mentoring Program

To create mentoring policies and procedures that ensure basic understanding of the program, consider answering these questions:

- How often should one serve as a mentor? Every year? Less frequently?
- How can mentoring be documented so that it can be used for relicensure credit?
- How different is mentoring from evaluation?

Administrators need to understand that mentors are not supervisors or evaluators of teachers. Mentors are selected to offer assistance and guidance to novice teachers as they transition into the professional educational community. The special relationship that forms between the mentor and new teacher is built upon fairness and confidentiality. Only when this trust is established and understood by both parties will the communication between them be maximized. Their communication is privileged and should not be used in the formal evaluation process.

Structures and Supports

When starting a mentoring program, it is important to distinguish between new hires who are also new teachers and new hires who are experienced teachers. Their needs are different. Create definitions for these different groups and provide different types of support.

In addition to time spent with their mentee, mentors need the time and opportunity to meet with other mentors and to work on problem solving. Similarly, mentees find it useful to meet with each other. Administrators are natural facilitators for these meetings, which should occur two or three times a year. While your group is designing the implementation of the mentoring program, you'll need to create a plan to sustain it. Creating a cadre of experienced mentors who can continue to provide professional development to potential mentors is key to sustainability, enthusiasm, and building a professional learning community.

Part of the preparation needed to become a mentor is to remind yourself what your mentors have done for you, what it felt like to be a new teacher, and the kinds of basic information you needed to start the year off without treading water. The following topics are the kinds of information that should be addressed within the mentor relationship.

SIX CRITICAL FOCUS AREAS FOR MENTEES

Novice teachers and mentors need to work together to address the following six critical topics:

1. Information—the nuts-and-bolts of a school and an understanding of the school's culture and climate. Included are such things as the policies and procedures of the school and district, staff lists, maps of the school campus and buildings and perhaps the local town, faculty and student handbooks, school calendars, lunch procedures, extracurricular duties, structures for community and parent involvement, school action plans, statewide professional development offerings, and contractual obligations.

2. Instruction—core knowledge and skills that teachers need in order to plan and deliver effective curriculum and develop teaching and learning activities in content areas. Examples include course guidelines, curriculum guidelines, goal statements, lesson and unit plans, curriculum plans, long-range general plans, modeling what is expected, Individualized Education Plans, supervision and evaluation processes, teaching and learning strategies, as well as standards, benchmarks, and rubrics.

3. Personal—how a teacher organizes and manages both personal and professional time to create balance and minimize stress. A calendar may include clues about time management, goal setting, health and wellness, stress management, celebration and recognition of successes, and self-reflection skills for revising next year's work.

4. Management—structures and strategies that teachers create in order to organize and run their classrooms. Management relates to class norms; procedures for classroom routines; lesson planning books; discipline procedures; budget and requisition procedures; referral procedures for the support team for special needs students; forms for referrals, attendance, and hall passes; grade book procedures; systems for tracking parent contacts; planning and organizing materials for state and local assessments; reporting end-of-year grades; and updating records and portfolios.

5. Results—classroom, local, and state assessments that provide information to the teacher, student, and parent regarding what the student knows and is able to do. This information is used to adjust or revise instruction to help the student attain standards or grade expectations. New teachers need to be familiar with state and local assessments, save samples of student work to use as future benchmarks, and create classroom assessments.

6. Collaboration—collegial relationships help teachers reflect on their practice for the purpose of improving student learning and teacher satisfaction as part of a learning community. For collaboration to occur, teachers need to set meeting schedules with a mentor and begin to form professional connections by sharing resources, discussing a professional article or book,

reviewing student work with another teacher or mentor, joining and participating in a professional organization, observing a mentor in the classroom,
helping with problem solving, and managing a crisis when necessary.

To assist potential mentors in continuing to build a context for their mentoring, use your own beginning teaching experiences to understand the six
critical focus areas for novice teachers. Working alone, you might consider
writing a description of the most pressing concern you encountered in each
focus area. Working in a group, mentors can write a description of a pressing issue encountered in each focus area (try a different color index card for
each topic) and small groups of mentors and mentees can then sort the
cards and discuss themes. The themes described by mentor teachers can
then be categorized into the six critical topics.

PHASES OF THE FIRST YEAR OF TEACHING

An understanding of the critical topics leads to sharing and discussing the
phases faced by teachers in their first year of teaching. See Figure 2.1, a
matrix that relates the six critical topics—information, instruction, personal, management, results, and collaboration—to the phases that a first-
time teacher moves through in a year of teaching—anticipation, survival,
disillusionment, rejuvenation, and reflection (Gless & Baron, 1996). With
guidance, mentors can identify the emotions and behaviors typical of new
teachers and learn to use the tools and strategies that best fit the new
teacher's development. As feelings, confidence, and behaviors change, mentors may need to use different tools and strategies. Timing plays an important part in the success of mentoring a new teacher. For example, asking a
new teacher if you can observe a lesson and give her feedback in October
might make the teacher uneasy. The same offer given in February may
receive a more enthusiastic response—after a relationship has formed.

   Although veteran teachers experience similar emotions (anticipation,
survival, disillusionment, rejuvenation, reflection) each school year, their
context is different because of teaching experience. When veteran teachers
are also faced with implementing new programs within a new context, such

FIGURE 2.1

Phases of the First Year of Teaching

	Anticipation	Survival	Disillusionment	Rejuvenation	Reflection
	First few weeks of school	First six to eight weeks of school	November and December	January–April	May–June
Mentor Focus	Set short-term goals Interact often Focus observation Interact socially Listen Engage in joint problem solving Promote reflection Provide support and encouragement			Peer coaching Problem solving Curriculum development Observations and feedback Collaborative action research Provide many options for growth Facilitate networking	
Information	Overwhelmed with information			Better understanding of the system and how it works	
Instruction		Overwhelmed by the need to develop curriculum (Even depending on unfamiliar prepared curriculum is tremendously time consuming)		Vacation is first extended time to organize curriculum and plan ahead Focus is on curriculum development, long-term planning, and teaching strategies	Think of changes you want to make for the next year
Personal	Romanticize role of teacher and the position Confidence Energy	Fatigued Lacking time	Begin questioning own commitment and competence Unprepared for criticisms from parents of students Own family members and friends may be questioning amount of time being devoted to work	Winter break allows normal lifestyle, time to rest, time with family and friends Sense of accomplishment	Begin to anticipate the next school year

FIGURE 2.1 (continued)					
	Anticipation First few weeks of school	Survival First six to eight weeks of school	Disillusionment November and December	Rejuvenation January–April	Reflection May–June
Management	Have idealistic view of how to accomplish goals	Consumed by day-to-day routines of teaching Spend up to 70 hours a week on schoolwork	Classroom management is a major source of distress		Think of changes you want to make for next year
Collaboration			Faced with first back-to-school night, parent conferences, and first formal evaluation		
Results				Focus on assessment as a means to ascertain student results and modify instruction	Begin to plan embedded classroom assessments for next year

Adapted from Gless and Baron (1996). *A Guide to Prepare Support Providers for Work with Beginning Teachers: Training Module.* Santa Cruz, CA: Santa Cruz County Office of Education, pp. 24–26.

as standards-based education, they often experience the same developmental progression that novice teachers have to work through.

SETTING CLEAR EXPECTATIONS FOR THE MENTORING RELATIONSHIP

At the beginning of the mentoring relationship, make a list of expectations to help clarify the mentor's role. Mentors can work alone to create a list of expectations and may choose to share their drafts with other mentors to critique and to refine their expectations for the mentoring relationship. Being clear about what mentors are expected to do enables focused interactions to take place, and precludes unspoken expectations that may lead to

---

FIGURE 2.2
Expectations of a Mentoring Relationship

Use the following prompts to help mentors think about the expectations for a mentoring relationship.

In our mentoring relationship, I will work to assist you with

- Standards-based lesson planning
- Time management
- Interpersonal relationships
- Procedures
- _____
- _____
- _____

We will work together to

- Reflect on our teaching practices
- Set meeting times and commit to them
- Honor confidentiality—our conversations are private reflections
- Solve important problems
- Learn from each other
- _____
- _____
- _____

---

confusion, frustration, anger, and withdrawal. Without clear and shared expectations, teams and relationships often fall apart, and the mentoring relationship is too precious to risk. Defining expectations should be partly the purview of the mentor and partly established by the school or district. Mentorship should not be completely idiosyncratic.

Some potential mentors are wary of sharing their expectations with their mentee. Urging these mentors to create partial drafts that they can review with their mentee often relieves their anxiety. Prompts such as those found in Figure 2.2 can be used to start profitable thinking and overcome the reluctance and reticence of new mentors.

Assessing the Relationship

Mentors need feedback that allows them to adjust and refine areas that can enhance the relationship. All learners need feedback to know when they are on the right track, as well as when to monitor and adjust their practices. Beginning mentors at Chittenden South Supervisory Union ask mentees to fill out a feedback sheet similar to the one in Figure 2.3 to get a read on the relationship.

The gathering of nonjudgmental data can identify teacher needs and serve as a source for instructional improvement. Establishing when to observe, in what context, with what intentional focus, as well as ensuring confidentiality, are essential elements that are described in depth in Chapter 4.

MONTHLY FOCUS CHART FOR MENTORING

Although mentoring is often practiced as a beginning-of-the-year process focused on logistics, it needs to be an ongoing, deepening, yearlong relationship focused on improving student learning. A structured calendar of guiding questions that probe the real purpose of the relationship—beyond, for example, communicating where the math department is located—lends a sense of security and stability to the mentoring process and reinforces the depth intended for both parties.

The Monthly Focus Chart for Mentoring (see Appendix), used by both the mentor and mentee, provides a working template for much of what a new teacher must accomplish the first year. The monthly calendar provides the mentor with a format that can be used to successfully support the mentee. The chart also acts as a template to use when providing initial professional development to potential mentors before they embark on their mentoring role. The calendar is not a prescriptive document nor a checklist, but it is a reflective framework through which both the mentor and mentee can give attention to the mentee's needs throughout the year.

Just as the mentor needs tools and strategies for a productive relationship, the mentee needs tools to help him meet teaching demands and professional responsibilities. The calendar format enables the mentee to stay on track during the year on six critical focus areas by referring to the template and using a series of tools for self-evaluation and reflection. The calendar serves as a vehicle to support and encourage reflection and self-assessment in order to improve teacher practice.

FIGURE 2.3
Mentoring Relationship Assessment

Dear Mentee:

Like you, I am learning more about being an effective teacher. Part of my professional responsibility is to assist you in developing your teaching and classroom management skills. Please mark the column that best describes our professional relationship.

Skill Descriptors	1 Excellent depth	2 Good depth	3 Not enough depth	4 Could be a future focus
1. Our interactions are developing into a positive, nurturing, and confidential working relationship.				
2. Our relationship includes being open to new ideas, methods, techniques, and professional responsibilities.				
3. Our relationship provides support and guidance in order to practice and learn new information and skills.				
4. Our relationship helps us recognize growth areas accurately.				
5. Our relationship provides for timely, descriptive, and specific feedback in order to enhance or improve practice.				
6. Our relationship helps us analyze teaching performance and identify alternative teaching strategies.				
7. Our relationship provides an opportunity to share effective classroom management practices.				
8. We meet regularly to discuss concerns.				

FIGURE 2.3 (continued)

Please suggest other areas, issues, and concerns that we can work on together.

_____

_____

_____

_____

_____

_____

_____

_____

_____

Source: Chittenden South Supervisory Union and Center for Curriculum Renewal. From Podsen and Denmark (2000). Copyright 2000 by Eye On Education, Larchmont, NY. Adapted with permission.

Many of the figures within this book are tools designed to accompany the calendar and help mentees organize time, manage their classrooms, craft standards-based lessons or units, and talk with parents about standards-based learning and teaching.

To avoid overwhelming the mentee, the mentor needs to be thoughtful about when he introduces the tools. Both partners can refer to the question prompts within the calendar to help frame the work for each month, but it is not necessary to use all of the questions. Similarly, when using the calendar, mentors might need to adjust or add questions based on local realities, such as the district's testing dates or district goals for instruction and assessment for the year. Mentors will have to consider whether or when to use a specific tool; the tools are a series of options for supporting effective mentoring relationships and effective teaching practice.

August: Getting Started

The month of August is a time for organizing. New teachers need to know basic procedures and policies of the school. See the Appendix to review what mentees typically need to know during this month.

Although mentors are sometimes expected to share the basic information, it is best to give new teachers a handbook and an associated checklist or to have an administrator discuss the basic information with all new teachers. That approach ensures that all new teachers receive the same information and protects the newly established mentoring relationship from deteriorating into a context of logistical issues. From the start, the mentoring relationship should focus on improved teaching practices designed to improve student learning.

Mentors can certainly support and repeat procedures and answer questions related to procedures. In fact, mentors may want to brainstorm informational issues (policies, procedures, and school rules) that might be useful to the mentee. Some schools use checklists similar to the one used by Chittenden South Supervisory Union to help new teachers begin their year (see Figure 2.4).

September: Management

Implementing a management system is key to creating the positive environment in which effective learning can occur. If necessary, mentors can share specific information about classroom management and grade books with mentees. Self-assessment by the mentee is useful to help confirm what is going right and to focus on areas of need. See the Appendix for useful questions for the mentee and mentor reflection this month.

Some fairly simple techniques and procedures from research and best practices are known to contribute to a positive learning environment in the classroom. The list in Figure 2.5 can serve as a guide for reflection and self-assessment, either as a regular review or as a means of solving problems when issues related to classroom management arise. This checklist also comes in handy throughout the year whenever a new classroom management issue arises for the new teacher.

In conjunction with the calendar, it is helpful to set personalized goals for the year. Figure 2.6 shows a template that can be used by mentors and mentees together to set goals for the year. The template is used to establish needs and priorities both for the mentee's initial teaching experience and for the mentoring relationship. Figure 2.7 shows an example of a completed assessment.

FIGURE 2.4
New Teacher's Checklist of Important Information, Policies, and Procedures

1. Building
   - ❑ Keys for building and rooms
   - ❑ Time schedule and access to building
   - ❑ Parking
   - ❑ Copy and fax machines
   - ❑ Faculty room
   - ❑ Cafeteria
   - ❑ Library
   - ❑ Main offices
   - ❑ Other student support services offices

2. Personnel
   - ❑ Administration, faculty, and staff
   - ❑ Team structure, such as grade-level teams, instructional support teams, special education teams, and 504 teams
   - ❑ Custodial and building maintenance

3. Classroom
   - ❑ Attendance procedures
   - ❑ Grading
   - ❑ Discipline referrals and follow up
   - ❑ Homework
   - ❑ Liability issues
   - ❑ Classroom and team procedures
   - ❑ Materials and supplies
   - ❑ Confidentiality
   - ❑ Dismissal

4. School Policy and Procedures
   - ❑ Sick, personal, and professional days
   - ❑ E-mail, mailboxes, phone mail
   - ❑ Student records
   - ❑ Substitute teacher plans
   - ❑ Textbooks (issued and collected)
   - ❑ Faculty meetings
   - ❑ Individual Professional Development Plans and professional development forms
   - ❑ Teacher evaluation
   - ❑ School handbook and school calendar
   - ❑ Fire drills and bomb threats
   - ❑ Assembly procedures
   - ❑ Field trips
   - ❑ Parent conferences
   - ❑ Snow days
   - ❑ Communication between school and home
   - ❑ Open house
   - ❑ Report cards
   - ❑ End-of-year procedures
   - ❑ Exams and standardized testing
   - ❑ Budget preparation
   - ❑ Confidentiality

Source: Teachers from Chittenden South Supervisory Union, Vermont. Adapted by permission.

FIGURE 2.5
Self-Assessment of Classroom Management System

The following rating system may be useful when using this tool for self assessment:

    3: I do this well and frequently.
    2: I need to increase my focus in this area.
    1: I need more information or support to do this well and frequently.

Connect with students

___ Talk informally with students about their interests before, during, and after class.
___ Greet students in and out of school.
___ Call students by first names as they come into class.
___ Be aware of and comment on important events in students' lives.

Monitor your own attitudes

___ Before class, mentally review students; note those with whom you anticipate having problems (academic or behavioral). Imagine those students succeeding in positive classroom behaviors—replace your negative expectations with positive ones as a form of mental rehearsal.
___ Consciously remind yourself of positive expectations when interacting with students.

Accept all students

___ Make eye contact with each student.
___ Arrange seating to give you clear and easy access to every student.
___ Provide students with opportunities to engage in cooperative learning activities.
___ Help students create strategies for gaining acceptance by peers.

Respond positively to incorrect responses or lack of response

___ Dignify responses.
___ Restate questions.
___ Rephrase questions.

Help students develop a sense of comfort

___ Frequently and systematically use activities that involve physical movement.
___ Periodically take short breaks that enable students to stand up, move about, stretch.
___ Set up classroom tasks that allow students to gather information on their own or in small groups using sources that are not at their desks.
___ Systematically switch from activities where students must work independently to tasks in which they must organize themselves in small groups.
___ As a regular aspect of instructional routine, use from 2 to 5 minute exercise breaks when energy levels start to wane.

Have students identify their own standards for comfort and order

___ Ask students to describe in some detail how they would arrange their personal space in the classroom. Have students create a checklist from their description that they periodically use to assess if they are keeping their personal space to the standards identified.

FIGURE 2.5 (continued)

Establish and communicate classroom rules and procedures

___ Generate clear rules and standard operating procedures for the classroom.

___ Communicate rules and procedures by discussing their meaning, providing a written list, posting the list, role-playing, or modeling use.

___ Focus on positive expectations—how people *will* interact with one another, not what they *won't* do.

___ Acknowledge changes in rules and explain reasons for exceptions.

___ Modify and adapt discipline strategies by asking what you could do differently.

Develop a sense of academic trust

___ Exhibit a sense of enthusiasm about material presented.

___ Link classroom tasks to students' interests and goals.

___ Ask students to generate tasks that apply to their interests and goals.

Provide positive feedback

___ Attribute students' successes to their efforts.

___ Specify what the student did that produced success.

___ Teach students to use positive self-talk.

Use classroom meetings

___ Bring up an issue or problem.

___ Give examples of and clarify issues and problems.

___ Identify consequences and norms.

___ Make judgments about norms and discuss values.

___ Discuss alternative behaviors and agree on which ones to follow.

___ Make a public commitment to adhere to the norms.

___ At a later date, assess effectiveness of classroom meetings and norms.

Use a conflict resolution strategy

___ List facts pertinent to the conflict.

___ Make inferences about how the persons involved were feeling.

___ Propose and defend own resolution in light of those feelings.

___ Describe similar experiences.

___ Describe feelings of each participant in those situations.

___ Look at other ways of handling the situation.

Supervise volunteers and paraprofessionals

___ Give clearly defined duties.

___ Enable productive and independent engagement to take place during the entire class.

Adapted with permission from Vermont Department of Education (1998); also some information from Joyce & Weil (1996) and Marzano (1992).

FIGURE 2.6
Needs Assessment and Goal Setting

Ask the mentee to generate questions or draft goals in the grid below; it's not necessary to fill in each cell. Here are basic questions to guide the responses:

- What do you wish you knew?
- What products or accomplishments do you hope for?
- What do you want to know better how to do?
- What dispositions, inclinations, and outlooks do you hope to exemplify?

	KNOW Information Concepts	HAVE Products Accomplishments	DO Skills Processes	BE Inclinations Outlook
Information • Policies and Procedures • Culture and Climate • Students				
Management				
Instruction				
Results				
Collaboration • Mentors • Colleagues • Others				
Personal Issues				

The mentor pair should discuss and explore the questions and goals together, identify the top three priorities that the mentee can accomplish alone, and determine the best processes to meet them. Then the pair should identify the top three priorities on which they can work together and determine the best processes to use to accomplish those goals.

The two need to schedule a meeting for reviewing progress, identifying next needs and next steps, and revising the goals as necessary.

FIGURE 2.7

Sample Needs Assessment and Goal Setting

Ask the mentee to generate questions or draft goals in the grid below; it's not necessary to fill in each cell. Here are basic questions to guide the responses:

- What do you wish you knew?
- What products or accomplishments do you hope for?
- What do you want to know better how to do?
- What dispositions, inclinations, and outlooks do you hope to exemplify?

	KNOW Information Concepts	HAVE Products Accomplishments	DO Skills Processes	BE Inclinations Outlook
Information • Policies and Procedures • Culture and Climate • Students			Contact language arts consultant to find courses or workshops or to recommend books and teachers to visit.	
Management	How do I do this in a heterogeneous class in a workshop format?			
Instruction	What do I need to know about higher-order thinking?	I want to improve instruction in critical reading and higher-order comprehension with my 7th grade students.	I need the pedagogy— questioning techniques, modeling instructional strategies.	I want to feel confident that I can support teaching of critical responses to text and that my assessments show that students have learned this.

(figure continues on next page)

FIGURE 2.7 (continued)

	KNOW Information Concepts	HAVE Products Accomplishments	DO Skills Processes	BE Inclinations Outlook
Results	What are the elements of a good assessment task for reading response?	I want to see improvement in students' thinking in their reading responses and book clubs.	I want to improve instruction in critical reading and higher-order comprehension with my 7th grade students.	I know how to craft a good performance assessment for a reading response and can use these tools to craft other assessments.
Collaboration • Mentors • Colleagues • Others		I would like to observe this in someone's class.	I would like to benchmark student work with another person.	I will be able to seek the advice of other teachers.
Personal Issues			Learn some tools for what happens if I fail—I'm not so good at risk taking.	

The mentor pair should discuss and explore the questions and goals together, identify the top three priorities that the mentee can accomplish alone and determine the best processes to meet them.

Priority 1: Calling the language arts consultant.

Priority 2: Reading some chapters on teaching heterogeneous groups.

Priority 3: Asking for help.

Then, identify the top three priorities on which the mentor and mentee can work together and determine the best processes to use to accomplish those goals.

Priority 1: Setting up a time to observe in a class where effective questioning techniques are used.

Priority 2: Looking at organization and management of book clubs.

Priority 3: Creating lessons to teach learners higher-order thinking strategies for making connections to what is read and finding evidence from the text.

Schedule a meeting for reviewing the progress, identifying next needs and next steps, and revising the goals as necessary.

We will meet every 2 weeks.

Goal setting for the year enhances communication and builds a road map for the mentee's articulated needs.

October/November: Instruction and Parent Conference

Usually by October or November, new teachers are ready to focus on enhancing curriculum and instruction. In many schools, it is during these months that the first parent conferences of the year will occur, and most new teachers value the opportunity to prepare and be prepared.

Lesson and Unit Design. Working with mentees on lessons and unit design is useful for both the mentee and mentor. Together they can refine instructional teaching and learning activities and assessments to meet specific expectations. For both the mentor and mentee, this is often new work. The mentee will find valuable questions related to lesson planning and reporting to parents in the Appendix.

An assessment plan is a design tool to help teachers craft what standards and expectations will be taught and assessed. The plan provides multiple opportunities for students to demonstrate attainment of standards or expectations and multiple measures that provide feedback to students. *Standards into Action* (Vermont Department of Education, 1999) offers a useful template for assessment planning. Figure 2.8 shows this template and Figure 2.9 is an example of a completed assessment plan.

Parent and Community Engagement. Many parents are confused by the use of new assessment terms such as portfolio, performance assessment, and rubric. Teachers can help them understand these terms by having real examples displayed in their classrooms. The best assessment and grading representatives are the students. The more students can speak about their own learning and achievement, the more likely their parents will understand, too. Using the chart in Figure 2.10 before parent conferences and with support from a mentor can help new teachers build a climate of acceptance for new assessment practices in the classroom.

December: Managing Stress

The Phases of the First Year of Teaching chart (see Figure 2.1, pp. 24–25) reveals that the new teacher may feel disillusioned in November and December. The new teacher is probably feeling stress from the

FIGURE 2.8
Assessment Planning Guide

Standards or Evidence	Instructional or Assessment Activity	What the Student Produces				Type of Scoring Guide Used				
		Selected Response	Constructed Responses			Answer Key	Checklist	Generalizable Rubric	Task-Specific Rubric	Observation Sheet
			Short Answer	Product	Performance					

Source: Vermont Department of Education (1998). *Standards into Action: Professional Development Toolkit for Standards-Based Education*. Reprinted with permission.

FIGURE 2.9
Sample Assessment Plan

Standards or Evidence	Instructional or Assessment Activity	What the Student Produces				Type of Scoring Guide Used				
		Selected Response	Constructed Responses			Answer Key	Checklist	Generalizable Rubric	Task-Specific Rubric	Observation Sheet
			Short Answer	Product	Performance					
7.1aa,bb,cc 7.12bb,aa	Cubes to Steam			written report and graph	experiment		X			
7.12aa	Density Investigation			written report	activity		X			
7.12aa,bb 7.1bb	Seltzer Bottles			lab report	experiment	X				
7.1aa,bb,cc	Falling Bodies		lab report			X				
7.1bb,cc,dd 7.12	Motion Centers			lab report	activities	X				
7.1dd 7.1aa,bb,cc	Marble Roll Balloon Rockets		graph and lab report		experiment	X	X			
7.1aa,cc,dd 7.12aa	Is Air Matter?				experiment				X	

(figure continues on next page)

FIGURE 2.9 (continued)

Standards or Evidence	Instructional or Assessment Activity	What the Student Produces				Type of Scoring Guide Used				
		Selected Response	Constructed Responses			Answer Key	Checklist	Generalizable Rubric	Task-Specific Rubric	Observation Sheet
			Short Answer	Product	Performance					
7.1aa,bb,cc,dd 1.5				poster	experiment			X		

Standard 7.1   Students use scientific methods to describe, investigate, and explain phenomena. This is evident when students:

7.1 aa   Frame questions in a way that distinguishes causes and effects; identify variables that influence the situation and can be controlled;

bb   Seek, record, and use information from reliable sources, including scientific knowledge, observation, and experimentation;

cc   Create hypotheses to problems, design their own experiments to test their hypothesis, collect data through observations and instrumentations, and analyze data to draw conclusions; use conclusions to clarify understanding and generate new questions to be explored;

dd   Describe, explain, and model, using evidence that includes scientific principles and observations.

Standard 7.12   Students understand forces and motion, the properties and composition of matter, and energy sources and transformations. This evident when students:

aa   Observe and measure characteristic properties of matter and use them to distinguish one substance from another;

bb   Provide examples of substances reacting chemically to form new substances with different characteristics, and describe and model the phenomenon with reference to elements and compounds.

cc   Observe and describe common forms of energy (e.g., light, heat, sound, electricity, electromagnetic waves) and their attributes, sources, and transmission characteristics (e.g., radiation, convection, conduction of heat).

Standard 1.5   Students draft, revise, edit, and critique written products so that final drafts are appropriate in terms of the following dimensions: purpose, organization, details, voice, or tone.

Source: Vermont Department of Education (1998). Standards into Action: Professional Development Toolkit for Standards-Based Education. Reprinted with permission.

FIGURE 2.10
Helping Parents Understand Assessment and Grading

Questions from parents about classroom assessment practices	Evidence that shows parents how well things are going in the classroom
What are the standards and evidence my child is expected to learn?	• Concise lists of standards, evidence, products, or performances for each student to master (in each subject area) are public. • Standards-based curriculum and assessment plan is easy to read.
Can you show me examples of high-quality work?	• Exemplars and benchmark samples of student work on typical classroom assignments, projects, and exams are displayed. • Students can tell their parents that the teacher uses lots of examples to "show" what is expected.
What are the standards of quality for student work? What are the expectations for this grade level?	• Expectations and overall evaluation plans are clearly communicated to students and parents. Information is sent home or is reviewed at parent conferences or on parent nights. • Explain that you cover expectations and standards at the beginning of an assignment or unit.
What are these new assessments that you are using? Do you use a mix of assessment strategies?	• Discuss the various types of assessments (e.g., classroom-based, state assessment, district assessment, standardized, standards-based). • Explain the different types of scoring guides and provide examples for each (e.g., answer keys for multiple choice, true or false, or matching exercises; rubrics and checklists for graphs, tables, diagrams, essay papers, lab reports, portfolios, projects, models; and observation sheets for presentations, demonstrations, and think alouds). • Display traditional multiple-choice tests, projects, presentations, exhibitions, performances, and essays in student portfolios.
Does my child ever assess her own achievement?	• Students see and understand scoring criteria. • Students evaluate their own performance on some tasks. • Students keep track of performance and overall progress through goal setting and portfolios. • Students are sometimes involved in parent-teacher conferences or participate in a student-led conference.

(figure continues on next page)

FIGURE 2.10 (continued)	
Questions from parents about classroom assessment practices	Evidence that shows parents how well things are going in the classroom
Does my child understand her own achievement and grade?	• Students can explain how grades are determined. • Students can identify performance descriptions and examples of excellent, fair, and poor work. • Student knows where she stands relative to what you expect in relation to standards.
What ways can you communicate to me about my child's achievement in your class?	• Possibilities include report cards, checklists, rating scales, portfolios, and student-led conferences. • Communication methods are sensible based on the information to be shared.
Some of these assessments may be biased and might negatively affect my child. How can you prevent this?	• You know how to identify potential problems and can determine the reason for concern and apply countermeasures. For example, a learner who knows the material but is a nonreader may score low on a multiple-choice test: You need to develop his reading skills or read the test to the student. Or, if the learner is emotionally upset at the test time and unable to concentrate, you may need to retest at another time. For students with Individual Educational Plans, the plan must outline what test-taking procedures or accommodations need to be made for classroom, district, and state assessments.

Adapted with permission from Stiggins & Knight (1997).

many demands from the six critical focus areas. See the Appendix for a few reflection questions for the month of December that can enable the mentee to maintain a sense of organization and possibly relieve some stress.

It is important to remember that there is not one perfect prescription for stress management. What negatively stresses one person may not negatively stress another person. The mentor should keep this in mind and not make judgments about the mentee's type of stress. It might be helpful to assure the mentee that there is good stress and negative stress.

• Good stress motivates, focuses, excites, energizes, challenges, creates opportunities, and is managed within the boundaries of motivation without debilitation.

FIGURE 2.11
Setting Priorities

When things arise that may threaten to disrupt your time, refer back to your priorities to see if the task, project, or request fits with priorities, is appropriate to do, will affect other tasks and deadlines, or can be given to someone else. Make a decision and stick to it.

Professional Priorities	Personal Priorities
What types of relationships do you want to build with coworkers? What steps do you need to take to achieve this?	What types of relationships do you want to build with family and friends? What steps do you need to take to achieve this?
What do you want to accomplish at work in the next 6 months? What steps are required to achieve this?	What are key quality of life issues for you?
What are your most important responsibilities at work?	What personal achievements are important to you?
What are the most critical expectations that your administrator has of you regarding performance goals?	

From *Time Management* by R. M. Hochheiser, 1992, New York: Barrons. Copyright 1992 by Barrons. Adapted with permission.

• Negative stress debilitates, causes lack of energy, health problems, low self-esteem, and chronic depression.

An area of stress for many new teachers is managing time. Finding a calendar that has room for all details of your waking hours is important. You can schedule both personal and professional obligations—from 6 a.m. to 10 p.m. if you prefer—and you can use the calendar to help monitor the extent to which you are or are not balancing professional and personal obligations. Mentees may find the priorities template in Figure 2.11 useful if managing time is an issue.

January: Reviewing the Long-Range Plan

Mentees begin looking ahead to curriculum expectations that must be met by the year's end. Managing content coverage, ongoing assessment, and refinement of teaching strategies are real concerns as mentees become aware of the number of months left in the school year. The questions in the sample calendar shown in the Appendix focus the mentee's attention on these issues. It may work well for the mentee to choose the questions on which he would like to focus with his mentor.

February, March, and April: Accountability

It is important for mentees to stay on top of assessment dates and the types of assessments that are given at the state and local levels. Test taking is a process that requires modeling and guided practice for students throughout the year—not just a week before an assessment. Procedures for accommodations and alternative testing need to be thoughtfully planned as well. Also, creating classroom assessments to obtain information on student learning for the purpose of refining instruction and giving feedback to students helps them become active participants in the assessment process. Questions in the Appendix address this task throughout the year. Teachers in different states need to revise these dates to meet their own needs in terms of both state and local assessments. The questions for mentees to review in February through April in order to prepare students and themselves for upcoming assessments are shown in the Appendix.

May and June: Endings and Looking Forward

As the school year moves to a close, the mentoring relationship also ends. Preparing for endings because goals have been reached is an important process. Planning something special to honor the relationship can enhance closure and encourage a maturation of the relationship when the adjournment stage is reached. Although there are many ways to honor the relationship and growth of both partners, it is important for the activities to be carefully planned. The activities can be as formal as leaving the school and going somewhere that has special meaning for the participants or as simple as taking turns expressing what has been learned through the work.

The calendar for May and June helps the new teacher prepare for the closing of the school year and in guiding thoughts about the coming year. Included in the last month is a reminder to the mentee to set up a time to meet with the mentor to share successes, and discuss what the mentee is most proud of and what will be changed for next year.

Mentoring provides benefits to both the mentee and mentor when roles are clear, goals are articulated, and time to communicate exists. Mentor programs can be one vehicle for helping new teachers become part of a professional learning community. In addition, mentor programs show support and respect to mentors who share their craft with others and continue to learn for their own development.

3

ORGANIZING
STUDY GROUPS

NEW AND EXPERIENCED TEACHERS USE STUDY GROUPS TO TAKE A DEEPER look at their teaching for the purpose of refining practice and improving student learning. Study group is a generic term used by educators to define a group of three or more faculty members who meet regularly to have a focused discussion with a specific goal that leads to improved teaching and learning.

Study groups do not appear spontaneously. Careful planning and trust building are important components of the process. There are various structures for study groups, each having a somewhat different purpose. In small study groups, teachers meet regularly to share issues, concerns, and dilemmas about teaching and learning. Resolving issues, finding solutions to problems, and sharing teaching practices for the purpose of receiving feedback are among the goals of different types of study groups.

When groups of teachers come together to improve their practice and thereby positively influence student learning, the results are compelling (DuFour, 2002; Elmore, 2002; Showers & Joyce, 1996; Murphy, 1999). Changes in professional practice often begin within a year's time and serve as a starting point for continuous study.

Focusing on curriculum and instruction is key to successful study group work. Study groups are cohorts of teachers who "reflect on their practice, challenge each other, together construct products related to their practice, and share materials, ideas or classroom observations that affect student learning" (Thompson-Grove, 2001).

CONTINUOUS STUDY: THE HEART OF FACULTY LEARNING

In study groups, adult learning and reflection are embedded into the work of the school. Shifts in professional learning become apparent as staff members

• Create a common language focused on an agreed-upon area of study. This is typified when the teachers within a district craft student assessment profiles in mathematics. These profiles paint a picture of student performance at three points during the school year. Through the selection of common assessments, the teachers are able to agree on what is being assessed and taught.

• Practice with new techniques, including those inherent in collegial feedback. For example, mentors in a New York district practice observation techniques, share observation tools and techniques, and discuss questions at mentor meetings to refine their skills.

• Share student work to solve issues and concerns. For example, English teachers in a central Vermont high school meet for two hours every six weeks to use a student work protocol to solve issues related to teaching practices. Substitutes are scheduled to allow teachers to meet during the school day.

• Refine skills and strategies initially introduced in professional workshops or courses. For example, the intermediate teachers within a Vermont district participate in a weeklong summer literacy workshop and meet four times during the school year to problem-solve implementation issues.

• Use data, often classroom assessment data, as feedback. Teachers use data to refine teaching practices during the year.

• Set targets for improvement. Teachers use data from statewide assessments, for example, to set targets in action planning.

• Celebrate success. During the January inservice meeting, a district celebrates progress toward successful implementation of a new reading program using midyear student assessment data. Streamers and finger food complete the celebratory feeling. Teacher evaluations of the event reveal how valued they feel.

• Start a new inquiry and begin the process again. For example, district teachers form a book club and read two professional books a year.

At the heart of faculty learning is reflective practice, a guiding principle of study group work. Reflective practice is thinking about your own actions before, during, and after teaching to determine if any changes need to be made to instruction and assessment. Teachers who engage in reflective practice are better able to support the reflection of others. Clearly, faculty learning is iterative and cumulative, and is emerging as a positive influence on professional and student learning. The impetus for faculty learning can come from a variety of sources, including school leaders or a small group of teachers. A state's program improvement office may serve as an external impetus that encourages a school toward a process of inquiry, usually with eye-opening results.

GETTING STARTED

The study group can include teachers, support personnel, and administrators. All study groups have a defined focus, ground rules or norms, clear meeting times, one or more facilitators, a structured process, and time lines. Most study groups focus their inquiry on student assessment data with the goal of improving student learning. Study groups can have a variety of configurations, although they may have overlapping attributes.

Creating group norms or ground rules is essential to the success of study groups. Agreeing on ways of interacting and communicating helps to ensure that the group works in effective and efficient ways. Chapter 1 provides examples of ground rules essential for group work.

Facilitation is a skilled responsibility and includes knowledge of the content at hand, as well as facilitation skills and appropriate facilitator dispositions. Figure 3.1 shows the attributes of effective facilitators.

Knowing the important elements involved in facilitating a study group can reassure novice facilitators. They can review the elements, assess their skills, and seek support and information as needed. Cofacilitation may be a useful support device for novice facilitators.

FIGURE 3.1 Attributes of an Effective Facilitator		
Content	Skills	Dispositions
Has a working knowledge base of issue at hand. Has a clear set of goals for session. Frames a problem or issue for assessment and action by the group.	Uses an inquiry process. Is an active listener. Paraphrases effectively. Creates an environment of trust and safety. Uses conflict resolution skills. Manages stress in the context of the session.	Is flexible. Uses intuition to test ideas. Creates collaboration. Thinks aloud. Remains neutral, but is engaged. Avoids judgment while expressing opinions. Admits mistakes.

Deciding on a facilitation format is another critical element for study group success. Figure 3.2 is an outline of three formats for facilitation: single, shared, and rotating. There are strengths and weaknesses inherent to all three; choosing a focus for the study group may help to determine the best facilitation format. Otherwise, the person most skilled in facilitation may influence the format.

Before embarking on a study group, determine the best size of the group and the time and place for meeting. Help the group focus on their responsibilities, follow up on needs, and plan for the next steps by keeping a log or action minutes. Chapter 1 offers a template for drafting action minutes.

Evaluating each meeting is important for revising and fine-tuning the purposes for the group's meetings and its goals. See Figure 3.3 for additional criteria for getting your study group started.

Using a set of criteria for planning the study group assists in creating a smooth beginning and a safe place to return to, if there is a problem noted by the ongoing evaluation process. Reviewing the initial criteria may prove useful. The issue of time can be used as a barrier that stops study groups

	FIGURE 3.2	
	Alternative Types of Facilitation	
	Potential Strengths	Potential Weaknesses
Single Facilitation	• Clear focus • Continuity • Predictability or consistency with respect to the group	• Out of touch with the group • Poor facilitation skills
Shared Facilitation	• Allows for greater insight while facilitation is happening; broadens the perspective • Provides a shift or focus in personality • Extends the energy of the facilitators	• Requires collaboration and consistency between people • Potential for mixed signals to the group
Rotating Facilitation	• Opportunity for members to develop facilitation skills • Shared leadership so that no one person has control • Everyone feels equally responsible	• Inconsistent leadership • Difficult for the group to build momentum • Requires clear group rules among participants about the role and responsibilities of the facilitator

from moving forward (Murphy, 1999). In order for study groups to take hold, the leadership in the school needs to think about how the finite amount of time in the school can be organized to support study groups. Consider the following:

• Review and revise the school schedule to find time for teachers to meet during the day for 60 minutes, either once a week or once a month.

• Set regular meeting times. For a data-driven study to have an effect, groups must meet often to share hypotheses, implement actions, share results, receive feedback, and refine and implement changes.

• If teams are part of the school structure, use team meeting times for study groups.

• Make substitutes available so that study groups can meet without worrying about class coverage.

FIGURE 3.3

Starting a Study Group

Use the following guidelines to get your study group off the ground.

- Set a consistent time to meet (a minimum of 60 minutes).

- Decide where to meet and what day of the week or month.

- Choose a facilitator type (single, shared, or rotating) or select the best option at the first meeting with input from all members.

- Determine the best size for the group, usually from 6 to 12 members.

- Create group norms or ground rules. Members must agree on the norms; use a round-robin group process so that every member is asked to agree on the norms.

- Use a log or action minutes (see Chapter 1) at every meeting to keep track of date, location, participants (present and absent), facilitator, actions to be taken (specify with whom and when), accomplishments of the meeting, agenda for next meeting, concerns, and issues.

- Serve refreshments at the first meeting and decide who will bring refreshments for each meeting.

- Consult the school and district calendar for conflicting dates.

- Ensure that materials are at the first meeting.

- Set a finite time line.

- Plan appropriate times for celebration.

- Establish an evaluation procedure and form for each meeting to help facilitators identify patterns, issues, and concerns.

- Work with school boards and communities to consider whether either early dismissal or late arrival for students is an opportunity for study group meetings. Consider the following options:
  - May we send students home early every Wednesday so that teachers can work in study teams for 1.5 hours?
  - May we begin school 1.5 hours later one day a week so that teachers can work in study groups in the morning?
- Use faculty meeting time for study group work and sharing.
- Use e-mail and chat rooms as a vehicle for study group interaction or for follow-up discussions.

• Give study groups choices about when they meet. Some may choose to meet before school, after school, or during school.

Leaders who believe in the value and potential benefits of professional learning communities provide the necessary structures and systems for study groups to thrive (DuFour, 2002). Before embarking on study groups, leaders need to assess if they are ready to support, encourage, and reward them. Figure 3.4 defines the leadership criteria for supporting study groups. Leaders can use the criteria to assess readiness for embarking on study groups.

TYPES OF STUDY GROUPS

Book Groups

> Marie, a 2nd grade teacher facilitating Chapter 9 from *Strategies That Work* (Harvey & Goudvis, 2000) shares with her book group how she applied the strategies for teaching comprehension of nonfiction. Marie tells the group how easy it is to integrate science (her weather unit) and reading comprehension. She says that the strategies work beautifully with her students and the students understand the conventions taught. She hands out copies of her lessons and explains that it takes several days to teach the strategies, but that the time is worth it. The book group members discuss how they each might apply the strategies to content they are currently teaching.

Definition. Book groups allow people to share ideas and opinions and to develop a common language and understanding for the benefit of the group and the students they teach. In this case, a group of teachers reads the same professional book and meets regularly to discuss key points. In a book study group, it is common for members to take turns facilitating the meetings. Book groups often focus on a specific content area that will help teachers improve their teaching and student learning. An expected outcome of a book group is the implementation of new teaching and learning strategies.

Organization. It is important to think about membership. Although book groups can be as large as 18 people, a large group makes it difficult for each member to have a chance to be involved and participate. If a large group is unavoidable, a skilled facilitator can orchestrate the discussions into small and whole group segments. The ideal size for a book group ranges from 6 to 12 people. The time and place for meetings depends on

FIGURE 3.4
Criteria for Leadership Support for Study Groups

Questions	Yes	No	If no, what actions can change this to a yes?
Does the leadership verbally and actively create time, financial support, and celebratory activities to support study groups?			
Are the leaders functioning as learning leaders?			
Do teachers trust each other?			
Do teachers feel respected in the school and district?			
Is inquiry embedded in the school culture?			
Is the focus of the study group clear?			
Is the study group an appropriate size?			
Are there actions and targets for the study group?			
Are data being used?			
Is there a clear process for the study group?			
Are training and other resources available to staff who need outside expertise to help them learn new instructional techniques, new facilitation processes, or new protocols?			
Is staff given 60 minutes or more during the school day for regular meetings (if appropriate)?			
Are teachers supported in observing a colleague during the day? (Often this entails the use of an observation protocol such as cognitive or peer coaching.)			
Will the observing teacher's class be covered?			
Are new teachers welcomed into the learning culture of the school?			

Some material adapted from the following sources:
DuFour, R. (2002, May). The learning-centered principal. *Educational Leadership, 59*(8), 12–18.

Kruse, S., Seashore-Louis, K. & Byrk, A. (1994). *Building professional community in schools*. Madison, WI: Center on Organization and Restructuring of Schools, University of Wisconsin, pp. 3–7.

participant preferences, although most professional book groups meet after school for no less than an hour. Some groups meet once a month and some meet weekly. It is important to set clear times, dates, and expectations for how much material will be covered at each meeting.

Sometimes book groups emerge from a restructuring effort and provide teachers with additional opportunities to discuss and learn more about the focus of the restructuring. At Wheeler Elementary School, a high-poverty city school in Burlington, Vermont, teachers were engaged in a restructuring effort with a clear data-driven action plan for identifying areas for improvement in literacy instruction for all primary students. Courses for the faculty focused on literacy instruction and the introduction of a book group to support the effort. Kristin Gehsmann, literacy coordinator for the initiative, devised the process for the book group. Each participant was responsible for facilitating one meeting, the time allotted to discuss each chapter of the book. The facilitator distilled essential questions from the assigned chapter, ensured that the group focused on the book, and summarized the three or four big ideas discussed in the chapter. Informally, the facilitator guided the group discussion, focusing in depth on one big idea.

Unless the book group derives from a small group of teachers who know each other, send invitations to all potential participants. The potential list will vary according to each school, book, and situation, but might include all high school literature teachers, all world history teachers in the school or district, or all guidance counselors. A sample letter of invitation appears in Figure 3.5.

School leaders often use incentives to encourage participation in a book group. Some schools purchase books for the teachers and tie the free material to specific expectations for attendance. Some schools give the book selection to every teacher and allow them choice about whether to join the book group. Other schools set up the book group and require participants to buy their own copies or seek available professional development funds.

Distance within a rural school district can make book group meetings difficult to attend. In Grand Isle Supervisory Union, a Vermont school district that covers 30 square miles, it seemed unrealistic for the teachers from the five elementary schools to gather for face-to-face meetings. To bridge the distance, the group decided to use the district's computer network to create

---

FIGURE 3.5

Invitation to a Book Group

Date: Nov. 28

To: All Bay Isle Staff

From: Kristin Gehsmann, Early Literacy Consultant

Subject: Book Club Opportunity

I am delighted to announce the return of our Professional Book Club Series. Like last year, we will be reading and discussing professional books together. Many teachers have told me that the club was the single best professional development opportunity of their careers. I'm very excited that we have been afforded the opportunity to continue this tradition at Bay Isle. All staff members are invited to join.

Together we will read and discuss two books. The first book, *Framework for Understanding Poverty* by Ruby Payne is a vivid explanation of the effects of poverty and the special considerations teachers must make when working in a low-income setting. It was a real eye opener for me! The second book is *Strategies That Work: Teaching Comprehension to Enhance Understanding* by Stephanie Harvey and Anne Goudvis. This book continues the work we discovered in *Mosaic of Thought*. However, unlike *Mosaic of Thought*, this book gives concrete examples of comprehension lessons. Both books are relatively short and easy to read. Your principal has copies of both titles if you wish to preview them or pick up a copy. Using last year's grant funds, we were able to purchase enough copies for all staff members.

Book club participants will be eligible for a stipend. Attendance at the following meetings is required:

January 7   *Framework for Understanding Poverty* (first half)

January 14   *Framework for Understanding Poverty* (second half)

February 11   *Strategies That Work* (Part 1—The Foundation of Meaning)

February 18   *Strategies That Work* (Making Connections)

March 11   *Strategies That Work* (Questioning)

March 18   *Strategies That Work* (Visualizing and Inferring)

April 1   *Strategies That Work* (Determining Importance in Text)

April 8   *Strategies That Work* (Synthesizing and Conclusion)

Meetings will take place in the staff room after student dismissal.

Source: Permission to use granted by Kristin Gehsmann.

FIGURE 3.6
Invitation to an Online Book Group

Join Us Online
for a
Professional Book Discussion Group
Lively Discussions for Improving Comprehension
and Enhancing Understanding

Who?   All K–8 teachers are encouraged to join the G.I.S.U. online book group!

What?   *Strategies That Work* by Stephanie Harvey and Anne Goudvis.

When?   Beginning Nov. 4th
Weekly online postings and discussions and one face-to-face meeting in January.

Where?   Cyberspace and the comfort of your own couch!

Why?   Comprehension is key at ALL grade levels. Through convenient online dialogue and *Strategies That Work*, we can hone our teaching for improved student performance.

How?   E-mail Wendy Cunningham at wcunninham@gisu.org to enroll.*

Criteria and Expectations for Participation

Complete reading assignments (about 25 pages per week) by Thursday.
Post one or more comments by Friday. Discussion prompts will be provided.
Read and respond to each other's postings over the weekend.
Attend one face-to-face meeting in January (time, date, and place to be determined).

----

*Enrollment implies commitment to all 10 readings and discussions. Upon completion, apply for LSB recertification credits (30 hours = 2 credits).

Source: Adapted with permission from Clare Sheedy, Grand Isle Supervisory Union, North Hero, VT. E-mail address is fictitious.

an online book group. Participants chose to work at home on the weekends and use a chat room for easy interaction. Each group member was assigned a specific chapter to facilitate and was responsible for writing a prompt that was posted on the site as a starting point for discussion. Figure 3.6 shows the online announcement; Figure 3.7 outlines the syllabus for the course.

FIGURE 3.7

Online Book Group Syllabus

G.I.S.U. Professional Book Discussion Group Syllabus
Fall/Winter

Strategies That Work by Stephanie Harvey and Anne Goudvis. (Stenhouse, 2000).
Copies can be purchased through Barnes and Noble online
$22.50 U.S.   ISBN: 1571103104

Sept. 16: Chapters 1 and 2 Strategic Thinking and Strategic Reading
           (pp. 1–26)
Sept. 23: Chapters 3 and 4 Strategy Instruction & Practice, Teaching with
           Short Text (pp. 27–50)
Sept. 30: Chapter 5 Book Selection (pp. 51–62)

Strategy Lessons and More

Oct. 7:   Chapter 6 Making Connections (pp. 63–80)

Oct. 14:   Chapter 7 Questioning (pp. 81–94)

Oct. 21:   Chapter 8 Visualizing and Inferring (pp. 95–116)

Oct. 28:   Chapter 9 Determining Text Importance: Nonfiction
           (pp.117–142)

Nov. 4:   Chapter 10 Synthesizing Information (pp. 143–167)

Nov. 11:   Chapters 11 and 12 Strategy Instruction in Context and
           Assessment (pp. 168–193)

Final Meeting: A face-to-face meeting (date, time, and location to be
determined by participants)

Source: Adapted with permission from Clare Sheedy, Grand Isle Supervisory Union, North Hero, VT.

Suggestions for Facilitation. Facilitation of a book group can be done by one person, two people, or a rotation system among members so that everyone serves as leader. Some book groups use a combination of facilitation types. For instance, primary teachers in St. Johnsbury, Vermont, used a combination model of rotating and shared facilitation for their book group. Higher-order reading comprehension was a major concern of the primary teachers, therefore the group chose to read *Extending Our Reach: Teaching*

FIGURE 3.8
Book Group Chapter Volunteers

Extending Our Reach: Teaching for Comprehension in Reading, Grades K–2

Date	Chapter	Cofacilitator	Cofacilitator
1/7	1	Linda	Alice
1/21	2	Fran	Peg
2/4	3	Juan	Jayne
2/18	4	Jeremy	Liz
3/11	5	Susan	Jen
3/25	6	Allie	Marcus
4/8	7	Allison	Sunni
4/22	8	Liz	Martha
5/6	9	Carol	Kathy
5/20	10 and 11	Brenda	Leroy

Source: Adapted by permission from St. Johnsbury School District.

for Comprehension in Reading, Grades K–2 (Pinnell & Scharer, 2001). To begin, a teacher sent an invitation to all K–2 teachers to participate in the study group. At the meeting, the group decided when and where to hold the meetings and who would facilitate. Figure 3.8 shows the chart they used to communicate facilitation responsibilities. The facilitating teachers were responsible for bringing food, presenting the material, and designing a lesson based on the material they read. During the study group meeting, the lessons were critiqued, revised, and distributed to all participants.

Kristin Gehsmann, a literacy coordinator in Vermont, suggests that each study group member keep a reader's notebook to record ideas he wishes to discuss or to use sticky notes to mark important discussion points. She also suggests selecting texts written by experienced teachers who have become researchers, authors, and advocates—for example, Calkins (1994), Harvey (1998), and Routman (2000). Their messages are often more convincing and tangible to teachers because they include practical classroom examples. Also, Gehsmann suggests selecting books that lend themselves to frequent discussion points and study over time, rather than choosing books that need to be read completely and then discussed.

Study Groups with a Problem-Solving Focus

A leadership team of teachers charged with developing a series of professional development opportunities on classroom assessment works with an outside consultant to develop a kickoff inservice meeting focusing on creating high-quality classroom assessments. In the beginning, the group is anxious and really wants the consultant to present the workshops, yet they know their colleagues will become more quickly engaged if they lead the groups themselves. The groups divide into primary, intermediate, middle, and high school committees. They spend three professional days within a month learning about classroom assessment and applying basic principles in their classrooms as they create materials for the workshop. They prepare agendas and design the facilitation process. Although the leadership team is apprehensive about the day and giving the presentation, the evaluations are the most positive ever.

Definition. Teachers meet to resolve a problem related to curriculum, instruction, and assessment using a structured, facilitated process. In our consultations, we have worked with several schools that want assistance in solving a particular problem. Some of the schools we work with are mid-sized, but some are so small and rural that the only way these schools solve problems is collaboratively.

Jay Westfield School is a small school in Vermont with one teaching principal and six teachers, including the special educator. The faculty was not satisfied with students' reading comprehension skills as revealed by assessment data. The staff wanted help with improving student reading comprehension, primarily in analyzing and interpreting text based on analysis of assessment data, and reviewing teaching practices as well as teacher-observation skills. With the assistance of a literacy consultant, the group crafted a professional development plan to work together to learn new reading comprehension strategies and observe some of them modeled by the consultant, and to process observations and practice the techniques in their classrooms. The consultant returned monthly and facilitated problem-solving sessions.

In addition, teachers developed classroom literacy assessments they used to chart progress and craft a literacy profile for each student. They implemented the profile and for the first time were able to use a common set of tools and language related to reading comprehension.

Another type of problem-solving study emerged in St. Johnsbury, a midsized school district that wanted to refine its primary literacy program. At the same time, the district qualified for a two-year federal project targeting successful early literacy programs. The school had four skilled Reading Recovery teachers who were part of the committee charged with finding a consultant to take on the role of literacy coordinator for two years. The school invited our consulting group to serve as literacy coordinators. As a result of this invitation and our belief that it is vital to inculcate these coordinators with the knowledge and skills to support classroom teachers, we served as external support to the staff. With our support, the four reading teachers practiced and learned the communication, facilitation, and planning skills that enabled them to be the literacy providers for all primary teachers in the district. The teachers were nervous about demonstrating guided reading procedures and strategies, therefore much of their work with us focused on clarifying roles and responsibilities, articulating learning goals, planning faculty meetings to debrief, and meeting to solve issues around resistance and communication. Success was further ensured when the district superintendent provided skilled leadership in articulating to classroom teachers that they all would be involved in learning how to assess the reading of K–2 students, use appropriate level books, and plan guided reading lessons to improve student learning.

To provide all teachers with the same knowledge base, the district sent the 25 primary teachers to Lesley College to learn the basic principles of guided reading. The teachers lived in the dorm for a week—bonding, learning, and questioning. Debriefing meetings were held twice to allow teachers to voice their concerns with external consultants facilitating these meetings. During this time, the four literacy providers also met with us to chart the work for the year. The literacy providers met once a month with our group to process their demonstration lessons, to discuss their relationships with teachers, and to continue to build their own facilitation and literacy skills.

The literacy providers prepared a monthly calendar to guide their interactions with classroom teachers. Figure 3.9 shows a sample of the literacy calendar that they drafted using the mentoring calendar in the Appendix as a template. The calendar format helped the literacy providers plan their work and be consistent. Teachers easily identified how the questions on the calendar tied to their instruction and assessment practices.

The literacy providers collected and summarized ongoing student classroom assessment and district and state assessments. Teacher evaluations and team meetings provided additional information on the progress of the literacy project. What first seemed like a problem for the district—finding an external literacy expert to drive the project—turned into a gift with a powerful solution. Skilled literacy teachers within the district were transformed into a leadership group that was charged with improving reading instruction. With coaching support from our consultant group, they created roles and responsibilities and charted a course for teaching and learning for all K–2 teachers. One literacy provider was quite nervous about her new role: "At first I was so nervous about what I had to offer and how they (classroom teachers) would receive it, but once we were in the throes of it—it was like one big group hug. It was so constructive." Three years later, the model has been refined to support primary teachers and now includes intermediate teachers as they look at their reading comprehension teaching practices. A classroom teacher receiving literacy support explained, "The modeling of direct instruction in guided reading groups—especially fluency—was helpful. The collaboration enabled us to receive support around instructional areas we identified."

Organization. The problem-solving processes used by Jay Westfield's small study team and St. Johnsbury's literacy team enabled them to craft doable solutions to their concerns. Each group organized around a specific focus, identified key players for participation, and appointed a facilitator to ensure that the work of the study group was complete.

Facilitation. A facilitator with strong communication skills leads and models the problem-solving process. If an external consultant has this role initially, administrators and lead teachers can learn the process over time so that they can facilitate as needed. Additional skills school leaders may need

FIGURE 3.9
Sample from Monthly Chart Focused on Literacy Learning

Colleague Support	Organization or Management	Instruction	Assessment	Professional Development or Collaboration	Personal
	Teacher	Teacher	Teacher	Faculty	Teacher
AUGUST					
Logistics Schedule meetings with each teacher for 3 months. Set ground rules for communicating. Create action minutes and keep them in a team notebook. Set agenda for faculty meeting. Decide how to divide up the library space. **Possible Questions for Teachers** What questions do these resources pose to you? Do you need help with the work board or scheduling? Discuss how to introduce the work board or order of icons.	Do you have books at needed levels? Do you know how to locate books in the book room? Do you have the materials you need to build a work board? Is your room organized for centers? Consider traffic flow, use of materials, display space, and storage. Is your room organized for group meetings? Do you have a simple schedule for the first 6 weeks? Do you have a management plan for the day—your daily schedule including 120–150 minutes of literacy time?			Bring your schedule for the first 6 weeks to the inservice meeting or faculty meeting. In quartets, discuss your schedules. In pairs, use a checklist to analyze your classroom environment for learning.	Breathe—you do not have to be perfect. Try this affirmation: I am a lifelong learner; a risk taker. I learn from my mistakes.

SEPTEMBER					
Logistics Do teachers have enough books at the correct levels? Audiotape a 1st grader reading; use this at faculty meeting for warm-up. Meet with 2 teachers and review their analysis of 2 running records. Create or buy templates for guided reading. **Possible Questions** What is the biggest issue facing you? What problems have you encountered? Where are you with these tasks?	Are you using your schedule effectively? Are you slowly introducing students to routines on the work board by modeling the task icon, practicing together, and praising them? Have you introduced students to the independent reading icon? Have you begun to create word walls?	Are you using the standard conventions of running records?	Have you set up a schedule for the primary observation study (POA)? Have you given the POA to 10 percent of your students? Have you analyzed the performance on the POA for those students?	Faculty meeting: Warm up with a running record of a student reading—record thoughts about fluency. Share how your introduction to an icon for the whole class is going. Start discussion about book collections for all grades. Record next steps on action minutes.	How are you using time? Who could help you with some tasks? What is working well for you?
OCTOBER					
Logistics	Do you have your guided reading groups organized?			Faculty meeting: Share your running record system with a partner; then discuss as a whole group. Review lesson management with group. Get feedback on lesson template.	

(figure continues on next page)

FIGURE 3.9 (continued)

	Organization or Management	Instruction	Assessment	Professional Development or Collaboration	Personal
Colleague Support	Teacher	Teacher	Teacher	Faculty	Teacher
NOVEMBER					
Logistics Have you scheduled meetings with 3 teachers for 3 months? Is everyone tracking progress on goals for guided reading? Do teachers have a guided reading template? Have you shared expectations for commitment to literacy with teachers in writing? Do you have signed agreements? Copy expectations agreements for each teacher. Place a set in team notebook. **Possible Questions for Teachers** What is the biggest issue facing you? What problems have you encountered?	Are any student behaviors challenging for you during guided reading? What might you do? Any referrals to Educational Support Team (EST)? Have you been keeping in contact with parents?	Have you considered flexible grouping?	Have you thought about or planned for POA in December? Have you thought about which 10 percent of the class you will assess on the POA? (Choose different children from those chosen in September.)	Faculty Meeting: • What's one thing that's working in your implementation of guided reading? • Let's talk about choosing the next book for guided reading.	How are you taking care of yourself?

DECEMBER

Logistics Administration of POA and reading recovery (RF) kids. Who will share how to go through book levels without teaching every book at the Dec. 7 meeting? Will we do text-level assessment for kindergarten? Plan how to schedule this assessment. What should be included in the calendar for the next 3–5 months. On Dec. 11, work with Nancy to continue drafting calendar. **Possible Questions for Teachers** What is the biggest issue facing you? What problems have you encountered?	How will you plan for the 2 weeks during the POA assessment, knowing that you might not be able to work with all groups in guided reading?	Which guided reading groups will you focus on during the first week of the POA? Which guided reading groups will be your focus during the second week of POA?	Did you assess 10 percent of your class using the POA?	Dec. 7 Faculty meeting: • Be prepared to share at least one thing that you are implementing with success. • Discuss choosing the next book, including use of chapter books and genre.	Come to the holiday party! Is your building party scheduled?

Created by the Center for Curriculum Renewal for St. Johnsbury School District. Adapted with permission from St. Johnsbury School District and Center for Curriculum Renewal.

to develop as facilitators include listening skills, interpersonal approaches (Glickman, 1990), and conflict resolution skills.

Peer Coaching Study Groups

In peer coaching study groups, teachers pair up to focus on improving a common curriculum, instruction, or assessment focus. Then they work with a self-selected partner to craft materials and critique implementation. Often peers choose to observe each other teaching a lesson and to share what they observed and learned.

> Directed and facilitated by the leadership, intermediate teachers in a district form coaching partners. The purpose of the partnerships is improved reading comprehension across the curriculum, a school action plan priority. Joan and Bob, a self-selected coaching pair, discover that many of their students cannot write clear summaries. Students confuse summaries with retellings and book reviews. Together, the pair develops a set of lessons to model the differences between summaries, retellings, and book reviews. Joan and Bob create criteria charts for a retelling, a summary, and a book review. They include on each chart a sample writing piece using the same content for each type of writing and agree to teach the lessons during the next two weeks in their separate classrooms. They will watch each other teach one of the lessons and will meet after school to discuss what each valued in the observations and to critique materials, lessons, and student learning based on classroom assessments they developed.

Definition. Showers and Joyce (1996) organize faculties into peer coaching groups with a focus on teaching and learning. Often the work is connected to an articulated implementation plan and a set of actions for school improvement. When working with whole faculties, teachers commit to participating on a study team and to planning, developing, teaching, and collecting data on implementation and student performance. In the peer coaching study team approach (and in peer coaching), teachers plan collaboratively, share lesson designs, and observe each other's implementation of the lessons. However, giving feedback, as outlined in the peer coaching model (see Chapter 4), is eliminated in the peer coaching study teams. A shift in methodology within the peer coaching model—eliminating verbal feedback—proves useful in effecting change in teachers' practice because peer coaching study groups focus on collaborative planning and group goals. Individual verbal feedback by peer coaches tends to undermine the study group collaborative process by making teachers feel that they are being evaluated. Removing verbal feedback keeps the study group cohesive and focused on the group's objectives.

Organization. This type of study team uses a collaborative approach to lesson design and implementation. The labor is shared throughout, as opposed to being a technical feedback process.

Facilitation. The process of working together to design materials and lessons is the heart of this approach. Although peers observe the lesson, they often just give advice, not formal feedback. The study team also decides how to monitor the change and the effect on student learning. The work of each study team must be ongoing and charged with skilled facilitation of the process, efficient organization, and focused work. A skilled facilitator provides prompts and frames for the collaborative work and helps the teams to solve issues and devise ways to evaluate the results of their practice.

Looking at Student Work

When teachers look at student work, they develop common criteria and common expectations. Together these increase consistency and help lead to improvements in instructional and assessment practices.

> A district's kindergarten teachers agree to use a writing assessment for narrative and response to literature writing. They meet two times a month to review student work and rate the pieces against a writing exemplar for each genre to reach agreement on the scoring of the student work. A facilitator leads the group using a specific protocol for assessing kindergarten writing. Teachers give evidence for their scoring judgments, discuss their reasons, and refine their scores. Over three months teacher scoring becomes similar. They start agreeing on writing pieces in the two genres that meet their grade-level expectations for the year.

Definition. Small groups of teachers use a facilitated structured process to review student work for a variety of purposes, such as improving student learning, refining lesson presentation, or benchmarking. In recent years, analyzing student work has been viewed as one of the most influential processes enabling teachers to reflect on their teaching and learning practices (Lewis, 1998; Graham & Fahey, 1999; Blythe, Allen & Powell, 1999; Seidel et al., 1997). A group of five to eight teachers uses a structured facilitated process to review student work.

Purpose. Structuring the method for analyzing student work is essential for successful conversation. It is important to determine the purpose of the investigation since there are a variety of protocols, each having a different purpose. Purposes for looking at student work include

• Understanding if student learning is meeting specific standards or moving toward meeting them.

• Creating student benchmarks for standards by agreeing on what high-quality work looks like.

• Helping teachers reflect on their teaching.

• Learning more about a student's thinking and learning needs and implications for instruction.

• Understanding learning needs for a small group of students.

• Helping a presenting teacher solve a dilemma or problem in instruction.

Facilitation. Although many different protocols may be used to address the needs of the teachers facing those situations, reviewing student work in a group is a useful tool that can offer targeted, pertinent professional development to a group of interested teachers.

The process of Critical Friends Groups (CFG) is a specific way of looking at student work, which is the core of the work by the National School Reform Faculty (NSRF). CFG is the organizing structure for looking at teacher and student work with the goal of improving student learning. CFG members generate well-crafted probing questions to initiate and sustain reflective thinking.

In Critical Friends Groups, teachers make public their practice for the purpose of receiving feedback. Teachers volunteer and participate in a group to obtain and share new perspectives, thinking, strategies, and ideas. Facilitators receive training in group dynamics and relationship and trust building, as well as in the use of specific protocols for problem solving.

After spending considerable time investigating Critical Friends Groups and committing to the process, the high school English department now meets every six weeks to discuss teaching practices. Ted, the trained CFG facilitator and an English teacher in the school, leads the group. Phyllis shares that she is concerned about a unit and needs some help. Although she has used the unit with success, six students in her 10th grade class are not motivated to analyze and interpret the text. Her practice is to use small groups to focus on a specific aspect of the book related to theme and author's craft. The work takes into account multiple intelligences. Four of the unmotivated students selected the same group topic, and she sees the "writing on the wall" if this group stays together for the duration of the study. She shares the book title with the teachers; two remark that they will use the book later in the year. Phyllis talks about the work involved, and five other teachers ask questions to further understand her problem. Then, Phyllis sits back from the group and listens as the other teachers provide new perspectives, thinking, strategies, and ideas. At the end of the session, the facilitator turns the discussion back to Phyllis, and she comments on ideas that make sense to her. Phyllis now sees how she can create a different iteration of the group work, as well as plan for whole group sharing. Phyllis feels rejuvenated and excited about the study. Two other teachers remark how this discussion helps their future planning, too.

Organization. Groups of 9 to 12 teachers, including administrators, meet either during the school day or after school throughout the year. CGF members meet once a month for one to two hours, and each group has a trained coach.

Members of CFG use student work protocols and peer coaching, as well as the National School Reform Faculty (NSRF) Consultancy Protocol (see Figure 3.10), to support teachers making public their practice for the purpose of receiving feedback. The intent of this protocol is to have the presenting teacher share a troubling issue about instructional practice, student learning, or curriculum. The purpose of discussing the teacher's problem is not to try to change or blame the teacher, it is to offer her options. The presenting teacher always has the last word regarding the conversations; building an atmosphere of trust and safety is paramount to CFG and the coaches that facilitate the groups. If teachers are to reveal what they feel makes them vulnerable about their teaching, then the level of trust must be high. Figure 3.10 outlines the consultancy protocol.

An important aspect of the consultancy protocol for the presenting teacher and the group is the use of effective reflective questioning techniques to delve into complex thinking. The National School Reform Faculty's guide to reflective questioning is shown in Figure 3.11. It offers good and poor examples of probing questions and possible question stems. The questions help group members formulate questions that evoke thoughtful answers by the presenting teacher.

FIGURE 3.10
Consultancy Protocol

A Consultancy is a structured process for helping an individual or a team to think more expansively about a particular concrete problem or dilemma. Outside perspective is critical to this protocol working effectively; therefore, some of the participants in the group must be people who do not share the presenter's specific problem at that time.

Time: 50 minutes

Roles: Presenter (whose work is being discussed by the group)

Facilitator (who sometimes participates, depending on the size of the group)

Steps:

1. The presenter gives an overview of the dilemma with which she is struggling, and frames a question for the Consultancy group to consider. The framing of this question, as well as the quality of the presenter's reflection on the dilemma being discussed, are key features of this protocol. If the presenter has brought student work, teacher work, or other artifacts, there is a pause here to silently examine the work or documents. (5–10 minutes)

2. The Consultancy group asks clarifying questions of the presenter—that is, questions that have brief, factual answers.   (5 minutes)

3. The group asks probing questions of the presenter—these questions should be worded so that they help the presenter clarify and expand her thinking about the dilemma presented to the Consultancy group. The goal here is for the presenter to learn more about the question she framed or to do some analysis of the dilemma presented. The presenter responds to the group's questions, but there is no discussion by the Consultancy group of the presenter's responses. At the end of the ten minutes, the facilitator asks the presenter to restate her question for the group.   (10 minutes)

4. The group talks with each other about the dilemma presented.
(15 minutes)

Questions to frame the discussion:

What did they hear?

What didn't they hear that they think might be relevant?

What assumptions seem to be operating?

What questions does the dilemma raise for them?

What do they think about the dilemma?

Members of the group sometimes suggest solutions to the dilemma; most often, however, they work to define the issues more thoroughly and objectively. The presenter doesn't speak during this discussion, but instead listens and takes notes.

5. The presenter responds to the discussion, sharing with the group anything that particularly resonated for her. (5 minutes)

FIGURE 3.10 (continued)

6. The facilitator leads a brief conversation about the group's observation of the Consultancy process. (5 minutes)

Tips:

Step 1:   The success of the Consultancy often depends on the quality of the presenter's reflection in Step 1 as well as on the quality and authenticity of the question framed for the Consultancy group. However, it is not uncommon for the presenter, at the end of a Consultancy, to say, "Now I know what my real question is." That is fine, too. It is sometimes helpful for the presenter to prepare ahead of time a brief (one or two page) written description of the dilemma and the issues related to it for the Consultancy group to read as part of Step 1.

Steps 2 & 3:   Clarifying questions are for the person asking them. They ask the presenter "who, what, where, when, and how." These are not "why" questions. They can be answered quickly and succinctly, often with a phrase or two.

Probing questions are for the person answering them. They ask the presenter "why" (among other things), and are open-ended. They take longer to answer, and often require deep thought on the part of the presenter before she speaks.

Step 4:   When the group talks while the presenter listens, it is helpful for the presenter to pull her chair back slightly away from the group. This protocol requires the Consultancy group to talk about the presenter in the third person, almost as if she is not there. As awkward as this may feel at first, it often opens up a rich conversation. Remember that it is the group's job to offer an analysis of the dilemma or question presented. It is not necessary to solve the dilemma or to offer a definitive answer.

It is important for the presenter to listen in a nondefensive manner. Listen for new ideas, perspectives, and approaches. Listen to the group's analysis of the question and issues. Listen for assumptions—both your own as the presenter and the group's—implicit in the conversation. Don't listen for judgment of you by the group. This is not supposed to be about you, but about a question you have raised. Remember that you asked the group to help you with this dilemma.

Step 5:   The point of this time period is not for the presenter to give a blow by blow response to the group's conversation, nor is it to defend or further explain. Rather, this is a time for the presenter to talk about what were, for her, the most significant comments, ideas and questions she heard. The presenter can also share any new thoughts or questions she had while listening to the Consultancy group.

Step 6:   Debriefing the process is key. Don't short-change this step.

Source: Developed as part of the Coalition of Essential Schools' National Re:Learning Faculty Program, and further adapted and revised as part of work of the National School Reform Faculty Project. Revised September 2001 for NSRF by Gene Thompson-Grove. Permission to reprint granted by Gene Thompson-Grove.

Critical Friends Groups are created only when there is a significant commitment from administrators, teachers, and coaches. Administrative support is essential in order for teachers to meet for one to two hours each month, usually within the school day.

Facilitation Format. Additionally, each CFG chooses a coach who receives extensive professional development. The CFG coach learns skills and strategies enabling group communication in an atmosphere of trust and support. In addition, the coach teaches the group questioning techniques, helping members to ask hard questions about practice "with care" (Appleby, 1998, p. 6). A primary goal of CFG is to break through the barrier of traditional norms about sharing practices or, rather, not sharing practices, in order to build professional learning communities. Critical Friends Groups are not formulaic structures; each CFG is quite individual, taking on the concerns that are important to the group and the individual participants.

Action Research

A university professor facilitates an inquiry with an 8th grade teaching team. The team wants to improve the critical reading abilities of students using fiction and nonfiction material from their integrated units of study. With assistance from the professor, the team devises an instrument to assess student learning before and after the implementation of new reading and writing strategies. In addition, the team creates reasonable targets for improvement. The facilitator provides the teachers with theory, research, and literacy techniques that teachers immediately apply with their students. Teachers collect data on a regular basis through informal classroom assessments and bring their findings and lessons to biweekly meetings, analyzing and planning next steps with the facilitator. The inquiry takes place during the fall and winter terms.

Definition. A professor facilitates and provides resources to a group of teachers interested in an inquiry related to curriculum, instruction, or assessment. The process is data driven and pursued throughout the year. Action research may take many forms. Calhoun (1993) defines three different types of action research.

1. Inquiry undertaken by an individual teacher.
2. Collaboration among a small group of teachers in a school.
3. Research involving all faculty in the school.

FIGURE 3.11
Probing Questions

The distinction between clarifying questions and probing questions is very difficult for most people working with protocols. So is the distinction between probing questions and recommendations for action. The basic distinctions are explained below.

Clarifying questions are simple questions of fact. They clarify the dilemma and provide the nuts and bolts so that the participants can ask good probing questions and provide useful feedback later in the protocol. Clarifying questions are for the participants, and should not go beyond the boundaries of the presenter's dilemma. They have brief, factual answers, and don't provide any new food for thought for the presenter. The litmus test for a clarifying question is: Does the presenter have to think before he answers? If so, it's almost certainly a probing question. Here are some examples of clarifying questions:

- How much time does the project take?
- How were the students grouped?
- What resources did the students have available for this project?

Probing questions are intended to help the presenter think more deeply about the issue at hand. If a probing question doesn't have that effect, it is either a clarifying question or a recommendation with an upward inflection at the end. If you find yourself saying "Don't you think you should ...?" you've gone beyond probing questions. The presenter often doesn't have a ready answer to a genuine probing question.

Probing questions are hard to create productively, therefore we offer the following suggestions:

- Check to see if you have a "right" answer in mind. If so, delete the judgment from the question, or don't ask it.
- Refer to the presenter's original question or focus point. What did he ask for your help with? Check your probing questions for relevance.
- Check to see if you are asserting your own agenda. If so, return to the presenter's agenda.
- Sometimes a simple "why ...?" asked as an advocate for the presenter's success, can be very effective, as can several why questions asked in a row.
- Try using verbs: What do you fear? Want? Get? Assume? Expect?
- Think about the concentric circles of comfort, risk, and danger. Use these as a barometer. Don't avoid risk, but don't push the presenter into the danger zone.
- Think of probing questions as being on a continuum, from recommendation to most effective probing question. Consider this example from a Consultancy session in which the presenting teacher was trying to figure out why the strongest math students in the class weren't buying in and doing their best work on what seemed to be interesting math "problems of the week."

(figure continues on next page)

FIGURE 3.11 (continued)

- You could have students use the rubric to assess their own papers. (recommendation)
- Could you have students use the rubric to assess their own papers? (recommendation restated as a probing question)
- What would happen if students used the rubic to assess their own work? (recommendation restated as a probing question)
- What do the students think is an interesting math problem? (good probing question)
- What would have to change for students to work more for themselves and less for you? (better probing question)

In summary, good probing questions

- are general and widely useful
- don't place blame on anyone
- allow for multiple responses
- help create a paradigm shift
- empower the person with the dilemma to solve his own problem (rather than deferring to someone with greater or different expertise)
- avoid yes or no responses
- are usually brief
- elicit a slow response
- move thinking from reaction to reflection
- encourage taking another party's perspective

Final hints for crafting probing questions. Try the following questions and question stems. Some of them come from Charlotte Danielson's *Pathwise* work (Educational Testing Service, 1999), in which she refers to them as "mediational questions."

- Why do you think this is the case?
- What would have to change in order for . . . ?
- What do you feel is right in your heart?
- What do you wish . . . ?
- What's another way you might . . . ?
- What would it look like if . . . ?
- What do you think would happen if . . . ?
- How was . . . different from . . . ?
- What sort of an impact do you think . . . ?
- What criteria did you use to . . . ?
- When have you done/experienced something like this before?
- What might you see happening in your classroom if . . . ?

FIGURE 3.11 (continued)

- How did you decide/determine/conclude . . . ?
- What is your hunch about . . . ?
- What was your intention when . . . ?
- What do you assume to be true about . . . ?
- What is the connection between . . . and . . . ?
- What if the opposite were true? Then what?
- How might your assumptions about . . . have influenced how you are thinking about . . . ?
- Why is this such a dilemma for you?

Here are examples of probing questions:

- Why is a stand-and-deliver format the best way to introduce this concept?
- How do you think your own comfort with the material has influenced your choice of instructional strategies?
- What do the students think is quality work?
- You have observed that this student's work lacks focus—what makes you say that?
- What would the students involved say about this issue?
- How have your perspectives on current events influenced how you have structured this activity?
- Why aren't the science teachers involved in planning this unit?
- Why do you think the team hasn't moved to interdisciplinary curriculum planning?
- What would understanding of this mathematical concept look like? How would you know students have "gotten it"?
- Why did allowing students to create their own study questions cause a problem for you?
- Why do you think the expected outcomes of this unit weren't communicated to parents?
- What was your intention when you assigned students to oversee the group activity in this assignment?
- What evidence do you have from this student's work that her ability to reach substantiated conclusions has improved?
- How might your assumptions about the reasons why parents aren't involved have influenced what you have tried so far?
- How do you think your expectations for students might have influenced their work on this project?
- What do you think would happen if you restated your professional goals as questions?
- What other approaches have you considered for communicating with parents about their children's progress?

From "Pocket Guide to Probing Questions" by Gene Thompson-Grove, Edorah Fraser, and Faith Dunne, National School Reform Faculty, Harmony Education Center, Bloomington, IN. Permission to reprint granted by Gene Thompson-Grove.

Organization. No matter what the makeup of the group, the steps of action research follow a clear order. Sagor (1992) suggests the following steps:

• Clearly define the problem in order to craft a set of questions to be answered. The problem should focus on teaching and learning. It must be important to teachers and worthy of their time and investigation. In action research, higher education faculty often serve as resources to suggest research to review, to provide professional development that might give insight into the problem, and to share research methods unfamiliar to the teacher.

• Collect data. Data collection takes many forms, including using existing data (e.g., achievement tests, grades, discipline referrals), and creating interviews and surveys. Sagor (1992) suggests crafting a matrix in which the research question and three sources of data collection are articulated. Multiple sources of data must be used to discern patterns.

• Analyze data. During this phase, data is organized into categories or broad characteristics that can be summarized.

• Report findings and action steps. Sharing the findings with other colleagues is important to the process. Using charts, graphs, and written text helps to articulate findings and provide insights that may occur only through the writing process. In addition, the research might generate new questions. Discussion with faculty using hard data helps to generate discussions about practice and builds a learning community.

Facilitation. Several weeks, months, or years can be spent implementing action research. Higher education or external consultants often facilitate the inquiry so that theory and practice can be more clearly connected. Essentially, action research is an inquiry process that uses a systematic approach to obtain answers to well-defined questions.

Whole Faculty Study Groups

Seventy percent of the students at an intermediate school are not meeting the standards in problem solving on state mathematics assessments. Their school is identified as being in need of program improvement. State facilitators and two independent consultants work with a small committee of teachers creating study groups for all faculty members of the school. The whole faculty participates in small study groups to find answers to questions related to problem solving in mathematics. Under the guidance of the state facilitator and consultants, school committee members learn action planning steps and facilitation skills that will enable them to facilitate each of the study groups. Committee members generate a list of inquiry questions related to mathematics problem solving that the study groups will use to investigate. Inquiry areas include content knowledge of teachers, mathematics program and curriculum, classroom assessment to inform instruction, course-taking patterns, groupings, student self-assessment, benchmarking, time issues, and professional development and associated resource needs. Study groups tackle one area apiece, generate research questions, collect data, and craft a hypothesis. They devise next steps and other types of data collection, making recommendations for actions on their topic. Each group takes action minutes that are posted so that all other groups are informed. The teams meet once a week for a month in order to generate action plans and receive feedback from other study teams on actions. The faculty prioritizes the actions and creates a time line for implementation.

Definition. Using an action research process, whole faculties form small action planning teams to craft their own goals, targets, and professional development. Each action planning team regularly shares progress with everyone in the school to facilitate the flow of communication. By design, whole faculty study groups involve all certified members in a school improvement effort. Murphy (1991, 1999) and Murphy and Lick (1998) coined the term "full faculty study groups" and they have written extensively about the process. First, analysis of a wide range of data is key to determining student needs, which become the focus areas. After prioritizing the focus areas, faculty members choose a study group. Study group work entails the development of an action plan.

Organization. Leadership clearly articulates that all teachers are involved in every aspect of the study group—developing an action plan within the study team, implementing the plan, and evaluating it. These groups meet regularly and may do some or all the following: design lessons; peer coach lessons; craft materials; learn new strategies; analyze student work; read professional articles, journals, or books designed to improve instruction; and plan needed professional development, whether provided by internal or external sources. Ongoing monitoring is key, with action plans being revisited monthly.

Facilitation. Murphy (1999) suggests keeping study groups that involve full faculty to six people. Each study group has a facilitator;

members share this role if they have strong skills. Study groups keep short logs, similar to action minutes, summarizing the work of the group. Group members are encouraged to keep individual reflection logs. Depending on each study group's action plan, a variety of different types of study may be used. Full faculty study groups may last a year or longer.

CONCLUSION

There are many entry points into study groups and faculty learning. For example, using Murphy's model, most types of study are incorporated into the yearlong work of full faculty study groups with each group using as many study group tools as appropriate for meeting the targets of its action plan. In contrast, schools may begin a study involving only a subset of the faculty. For example, primary teachers at St. Johnsbury School refined their literacy instruction and assessment by attending a course together, using lead teachers and literacy support providers to demonstrate lessons and work with each teacher during literacy instruction. Inservice meetings, faculty meetings, and team meetings served to refine and reflect on practice. Then, during the next year of implementation, book groups began to emerge along with a protocol for looking at student work. Now in their third year, the model involves the intermediate grades.

Other schools start Critical Friends Groups when one teacher with an interest in this type of study receives professional development in skilled facilitation and begins the process with a group of committed colleagues. Figure 3.12 provides a list of study group possibilities and an overview of reflective practice.

Creating learning communities in which learning and teaching are the ongoing work of administrators and faculty changes relationships, teacher practices, and student learning in positive ways. The learning of many can transform a school. The words of this St. Johnsbury teacher reveal the power of study groups and professional learning: "It gave me a chance to learn and grow in my teaching."

Leadership commitment is needed to support learning communities. In Chapter 4 you'll find an in-depth focus on the role of leadership in guiding and supporting professional learning communities through coaching.

FIGURE 3.12
Reflective Practice

Teachers who engage in reflective practice are better able to support the reflection of others. Reflective practice is a guiding principle of study group work.

What is reflective practice?	Reflective practice is thinking about one's own actions before, during, and after teaching to determine if any changes need to be made to instruction and assessment. Reflective practice can be personal reflection or reflecting by talking with another person.
How can reflection help teachers to improve their teaching?	Reflective practice helps teachers • See more than one way of being and acting in situations. • Understand why they respond or do not respond in a classroom situation and give reasons for response. • Seek resources, including peers, when other perspectives are needed. • Use reflective practice or model (for students) how to be reflective. This can help students to cultivate reflective dispositions toward learning.
Reflective Practices	
Individual or Interactive Journal Writing or Logs	Journals nurture reflection. Thoughts of both mentor and mentee can be written in a short form to recall events that can lead to further discussion. Journals and journal dialogues are useful, but make sure ground rules are established for sharing: Who gets to read the journal and what is to be done with the information.
Cognitive Coaching	Cognitive Coaching includes a preconference, a lesson observation, and a postconference. The coach supports teacher self-assessment through a Socratic dialogue (Sparks, 1990).
Peer Coaching	Peer coaching includes a preconference, a lesson observation, and a postconference. There are at least two rounds of peer coaching. The variety of peer coaching includes: mirroring (observe, record, no interpretation), collaborative coaching (transfer of skill or strategies to classroom practice), expert coaching, coach as mentor (giving direct, specific feedback to improve student performance).

(figure continues on next page)

FIGURE 3.12 (continued)	
Study Groups	Study groups come together for a specific time period to discuss professional issues, review a shared article or book, and to research a specific problem to pose solutions. Study groups have many configurations—the most common are listed below.
Book Club Study Groups	Book clubs include two or more teachers who read a professional book with the purpose of learning more about teaching and learning in a specific area. Book groups meet weekly or monthly, often after school; they meet either in person or online.
Problem-Solving Study Groups	Problem-solving groups use a specific problem-solving process to solve an issue important to the group.
Peer Coaching Study Groups	Peer coaching study groups involve pairs of teachers focusing on a question related to instructional practices, materials, or management and organization issues. Teachers address their inquiry by researching literature, applying new practices, observing each other teach, making materials together, and giving informal feedback to each other about implementation of materials, strategies, and learning.
Looking at Student Work Study Groups	Looking at student work involves a protocol, or steps for reviewing the work. Purposes for the reviewing work include setting benchmarks, determining if students are moving toward or attaining standards, helping teachers reflect on their teaching, and learning more about student thinking.
Critical Friends Groups	A Critical Friends Group is a structure created by the National School Reform Faculty in which small groups of teachers (8–12) are led by a highly trained coach and use structured formats (such as Consultancy Protocol and student work protocols) with the ultimate goal of improving practice and student learning.
Action Research Study Groups	Action research uses the following inquiry process systematically to answer a question. It can be used by an individual teacher, a group of teachers, or a whole faculty. The action research process includes 1) defining a problem and research questions, 2) collecting data, 3) analyzing data, and 4) reporting findings and action steps.
Whole Faculty Study Groups	Whole faculty study groups involve all certified faculty members in a school improvement effort. Faculty members join small groups, use a problem-solving process, collect and analyze data, set goals, and develop an action plan that they implement and evaluate.

4

COACHING

CURRENT EDUCATIONAL LITERATURE ON CHANGE AND IMPROVED STUDENT learning is clear: Schools must create opportunities for leaders, leadership teams, and teachers to engage in learning through collaborative opportunities. These collaborative opportunities enhance practice, teacher satisfaction, and student learning (Elmore, 2002; Fullan, 2002; Joyce & Calhoun, 1998).

Collaborative practices are still not the norm in all schools, although pockets of schools are using collaborative learning models. Unfortunately, professional development is often limited to inservice days spread throughout the year and graduate courses offered after school or in the summer. The notion that teachers belong in the classroom every hour of the school day, isolated from their colleagues, will not lead to the kinds of classrooms needed to improve the learning of all students in significant ways.

How can schools develop the kind of environment that supports adult learning and teaching, thereby improving opportunities for student learning? Investing in coaching is one way to build toward collaborative adult learning. Coaches relate as partners, not as experts, authorities, or healers. Coaching relationships flourish when they are based on trust—when the connection between two colleagues feels right. Essential to the relationship are the skills and tools that coaches bring to the partnership:

- Listening without judgment.
- Observing in classrooms and describing what is seen.

- Using techniques to build trust within the coaching relationship.
- Honoring confidentiality.
- Supporting reflections using open-ended questions or Socratic dialogue.
- Eliciting solutions and strategies from the person being coached.
- Using data to set goals, analyze issues, and measure success.
- Using communication strategies to promote thinking and learning.

A coach's job is to support and enhance the school leader's skills, resources, and creativity. The coach provides a focus and supports learning that the leader is not likely to do alone. Leadership coaching and peer coaching offer schools opportunities for cultivating job-embedded professional development, which ultimately serves all learners—both the adults and the students they teach. With a focus on reflection, content, practice, and relationship, coaching can help leaders and teachers improve student learning and overall satisfaction within the professional learning community.

LEADERSHIP COACHING

School leaders can use coaching as a way to make the changes necessary so that both teachers and students are learners performing at high levels. Given coaching support, curriculum directors, principals, and superintendents can enhance their leadership skills and find answers to their unique needs. A leadership coach can help a leader broaden her understanding of the education change process, including its complexities and challenges. A coach can help a leader attain skills and strategies that can transform a school into a high-quality school.

Leadership coaches can support veteran leaders concerned about school improvement, as well as novice leaders and leadership teams. In addition, as school districts become increasingly aware of the need for supporting the development of leaders within the teaching ranks, they are creating jobs with titles such as teachers on assignment, literacy support providers, mathematics teacher leaders, data coaches, and science coordinators. Talented, motivated, creative, and hard-working classroom teachers are taking on these new positions and seeking support as they try to learn what their job descriptions really mean and what skills they need to successfully attain their goals. Leadership coaches can provide the support and skills that can assist these new leaders. One novice aptly describes the skills, knowledge, and dispositions that she needed during the first year in her position as the literacy leader:

> I was excited to be hired as the district's first literacy coordinator. But I just had come out of the classroom and there was so much to learn! My charge was to assist teachers in helping K–3 students become better readers. Data were used to determine growth. There was a lot I didn't know about systems change, leadership, styles of communication, and content. My coach really helped me to focus and learn as fast as I could. Our weekly meetings, sometimes in the district office and often in my living room, really helped me to connect with my coach. We had a relationship based on trust, and that fostered a positive learning environment. I needed to learn systems for communicating across a district that had five schools in a 30-mile radius. I learned to take action minutes, set time lines, create agendas with a new literacy council, and develop timely methods to disseminate minutes and information about actions that were designed to improve teaching and learning.
>
> And I learned content. I needed to build on what I already knew about literacy. My coach gave me numerous books to read and suggested conferences to attend. These professional development activities allowed me to network with people who had more knowledge in literacy than I did—and I learned much from these connections.
>
> I learned along with the literacy council. We learned by reading, using protocols for student work, and creating workshops based on our data and teacher requests. We became a learning team, often having conversations on the run during school and after school.
>
> I've learned how to give presentations to other administrators in the district and to the school board. I am refining my communication, organization, relationship, and content skills on my own now. I have contracted with my coach to continue supporting me for a few days this year so that I don't get totally derailed. I know my coach knows how to help.

Leadership coaches work with seasoned and novice leaders who are interested in looking at their own practices with the goal of improvement and enhancement of their leadership capabilities. Consultants often serve as coaches to principals and curriculum directors. One novice principal interested in improving reading comprehension in her school realized that not all teachers in the building had a common understanding of reading comprehension. Although the principal had a clear goal, she had no idea where to start. With consultation and conversation with her coach, she was able to devise a plan that enabled teachers to see demonstrations of best practices for reading comprehension and to attend four half-day seminars throughout the year to process and solve problems related to the new learning. A reading specialist was contracted to lead this work. The principal and the teachers learned together and built a common language and a set of strategies for improving reading comprehension. Occasionally, the principal would phone her coach to discuss ideas and next steps.

In another leadership consultation, we served as coaches for a curriculum director in a school district. The superintendent was concerned that the school board might perceive the coaching contract as an indication that the curriculum director lacked competence. A simple change in contract language from "coaching" to "consultation" resolved the issue. The language is not important. The key is the nature of the interaction, the presence of ongoing support, and the opportunity to call on someone else's expertise when needed.

Leadership coaching can assist in uncovering a person's leadership abilities. Coaching can assist leaders in reaching educational goals and in making the connection between what they do and how that affects the other people in the school. Coaches can help leaders reflect on their actions and be conscious of processes that they are using to move their schools forward.

Focusing the Coaching Relationship

Developing a person's leadership capacity is a complex process and should start by determining what aspects of the person's professional role will benefit most from working with a coach. We've used Michael Fullan's (2001) concept of the core capacities that leaders need to develop as a framework for goal setting for the leader; the framework can also be the focus for working with a coach.

Moral Purpose. Leaders with moral purpose care about their schools and are driven to seek high performance from all students and teachers. They are steadfast, trustworthy, and have moral convictions.

Change Process. Understanding the change process, with its bumps, is essential for a leader. Realizing that morale will decline during the first year of change helps leaders to support the organization. Some insight into the different leadership styles that serve to move the organization forward during the change process is also helpful. For example, Goleman (2000) identifies these leadership styles that positively serve organizations:

Coaching style: Cultivates others in the school to serve in leadership capacities.

Affiliative style: Creates interpersonal connections and focuses only on the needs of the group.

Democratic style: Solicits input to form shared understanding and initiative.

Pacesetting style: Leads by example and expectations—action is more powerful than words.

Trust Building. By working to gain and maintain trust through relationship building, the change efforts can continually move forward. Leaders must be able to analyze and monitor their own actions and reactions in order to understand the actions and reactions of others. Leaders who understand relationships cultivate high levels of emotional intelligence, are empathetic, and have strong social skills.

Knowledge Building. Building knowledge and sharing it with others is imperative for lasting change. People must have opportunities to share and build knowledge. Leaders must enable knowledge building on a regular and ongoing basis.

Coherence Making. While change is occurring, people often feel confused and fragmented. It is important that leaders work to build meaning and coherence in the midst of change.

A leadership coach can provide support to leaders as they work to cultivate these capabilities. Figure 4.1 provides a self-assessment and goal-setting tool for prioritizing areas for consideration when administrators and teacher leaders are working with a leadership coach.

FIGURE 4.1

Leadership Goal Setting:
Setting Priorities for Working with a Coach

Step 1. Using Fullan's framework for leadership, read each of the core capabilities and question prompts and write a reflection on each area.

Core Capabilities*	Reflective Questions for Inquiry
1. Having a Clear Moral Purpose	What drives me to make a positive difference with teachers, students, and communities?
	Do I need to make changes in the environment for the better? Have I? In what ways?
	How am I helping to close the gap between high-achieving students and low-achieving students (in literacy, mathematics, science, social studies)?
	How am I committed to systemic improvement in my school and all schools in the district? What am I doing to help make this happen?
2. Understanding the Change Process	How many innovations do I have going? Have I focused my energy on a reasonable number of changes?
	Have I decreed the change and demanded that people follow it? Have I worked with others to build meaning and support for the change?
	Do I really understand what an implementation dip means? Can I sustain and support people during the first year when the going is tough? What do I need to know about the implementation dip?
	How do I deal effectively with doubters and naysayers? What skills do I need to work with these people?
	Am I supporting a new school culture? Are people talking about and valuing what we are changing? Are people working together differently? Do I provide opportunities for them to discuss the change, look at our practice, and visit schools working on similar changes? Or am I just changing titles, roles, and responsibilities?

FIGURE 4.1 (continued)	
Core Capabilities*	**Reflective Questions for Inquiry**
3. Building Positive Relationships	Do I build relationships with diverse people or people who think just like me? Am I authentic? Do I care about the people I relate to?
	Am I supporting the development of professional learning communities? Does professional development include everyone—not just particular teams or teachers?
	Do I hold people accountable for their contributions to our goals?
	Am I self-aware? Do I observe my emotional states and manage them? Do I have empathy, good social skills, what it takes to inspire and motivate others? Do I vary my leadership style as needed?
4. Making Knowledge Sharing a Cultural Value	Do I provide opportunities for action research, study groups, or inquiry groups in small meetings and with larger groups?
	Do I make knowledge gathering and learning a social process where people share openly what they are learning?
	Do I enable people to increase their knowledge inside and outside the organization?
5. Making Coherence for Self and Others in the Midst of Overload and Fragmentation	Am I adapting to the complexity that occurs with change, and can I maintain focus while seeking solutions and coherence?
	Do I help my faculty examine student performance data and make critical sense of the information? Do I help faculty disaggregate data? Do I encourage faculty to hypothesize about patterns to help make sense of confusion? Do I help my faculty create action plans based on data that we can use for coherence building?

(figure continues on next page)

FIGURE 4.1 (continued)

Step 2. Prioritize the 5 core capabilities.

1.

2.

3.

4.

5.

Step 3. Which core capabilities will you focus on with a coach? What can you investigate and reflect on by yourself? How might you put these ideas into practice?

Step 4. For those priorities you will explore with a coach, draft goals, a time line, a plan, and how you might assess your progress. Use these items as a springboard for conversation with your coach.

Focus:

Goals:

Time line (think 6 months, 1 year, 2 years):

Plan: How will you know when you've met short-term and long-term goals?

---

*These five core capabilities are adapted from Fullan, M. (2001). *Leading in a Culture of Change*. San Francisco, CA: Jossey-Bass. Copyright 2001 John Wiley & Sons, Inc. Adapted with permission.

	Advantages	Disadvantages
FIGURE 4.2 **Choosing an "Outside" Coach or an "Inside" Coach**		
Coach from outside the school	Insight into the culture of the organization from an outsider's perspective. Expertise, references, and past successes. Specifies contracted meeting times. Can choose to be confidential. Seen as strength by school board.	May be a mismatch in style and beliefs about leadership. Expense. Seen as a weakness by school board.
Coach from inside the school	Familiar with the culture of the school. Can assist in building a culture around coaching. Less expensive. Compatible. On-site; can be accessed easily. May have strong skills or be willing to refine them.	Too close to the organization to be objective. May have biases about culture and school personnel. Meeting times must be juggled because of other responsibilities. Weak coaching skill set.

Choosing a Coach

Accessing a coach within the leader's environment may be an asset or a liability. The school's environment may dictate whether you should choose a coach inside or outside your school or district. Consider these questions:

• Do you feel comfortable having other people know that you are using a coach?

• Would you prefer a coach from outside your school district because of the perspective he might offer?

• Do you want to work with coach within your school or district to build or promote a culture of coaching?

An overview of the advantages and disadvantages of choosing a coach from inside or outside your school or district is offered in Figure 4.2.

FIGURE 4.3
Framework for Selecting a Leadership Coach

Personal Attributes	Practical Experience	Skills
Can the coach tell you what she feels coaching has done for her?	Is this person capable at what she does?	Does this person engender trust in others?
Does this person communicate effectively with you? How does she interact with you?	Has the person been successful at coaching other people? Ask for examples.	Does this person have skills dealing with conflict, working with groups, communicating effectively across a variety of different audiences?
Is this person respected for her opinion and do people seek her expertise?	Does the coach have a variety of practical experiences combined with the ability to explain or demonstrate principles of success?	Does this person have an understanding of change processes, standards-based curriculum, instruction and assessment, and how to develop learning communities?
Is this person positive and supportive in her outlook?		

After deciding whether the coach will be someone from inside or outside your school or district, the next step is to create a list of attributes for selecting your coach. See Figure 4.3 for guidance. Working with someone who has practical experience related to your responsibilities and who is also a capable coach is essential. It is important to find out how often the potential coach has been successful at coaching other people. When interviewing a coach, ask for specific examples of her successes. Asking the coach what she feels coaching has done for her is another inquiry certain to be informative. Asking for references, talking with people she has coached, and asking specifically about trust can reveal valuable information. Observe whether the person is positive and supportive in her outlook. Through interviewing, ascertain whether the coach has a variety of practical experiences combined with the ability to explain or demonstrate principles of success. Also, determine whether the coach is skilled in dealing with conflict, working with groups, and communicating effectively across a variety of audiences.

PEER COACHING

Just as leadership coaches support administrators and teacher leaders, peer coaches are teachers helping teachers refine their practice. Peer coaching began as a way to improve the application of new teaching practices after initial staff development training (Joyce & Showers, 1983). Since the 1980s, peer coaching has continued to evolve. Peer coaching is a partnership that can assist teachers in the improvement of instruction by engaging in the study of the teaching craft and builds collegiality among pairs of teachers. Focusing on instructional practice is complex and "requires people to operate in networks of shared and complementary expertise" (Elmore, 2002, p. 24).

In peer coaching, colleagues observe and coach each other using a defined protocol for planning a focus prior to the agreed-upon teacher demonstration. It is similar to the supervisory evaluation process of preconference, observation, and postconference, but it takes place between two collegial teachers and is never used for contractual summative evaluation purposes. Specifically, peer coaching is used to inform practice for the purpose of improving student learning. Peer coaching can be useful when colleagues use it to refine instructional strategies; implement a new instructional strategy; or to solve problems in classroom management, instruction, or assessment. Figure 4.4 summarizes the purposes of peer coaching.

Peer coaching can be used when one colleague is more expert in a particular instructional strategy and is supporting another colleague's implementation of that strategy. Here is a teacher's reflection on the value of observing a demonstration lesson by an experienced colleague:

> As a kindergarten teacher and part of a primary team, I was being pressured by my colleagues to participate in an early literacy learning conference where they hoped I would embrace teaching literacy learning in kindergarten. I had always taught a social type of kindergarten, which my

> ## FIGURE 4.4
> ### Purposes of Peer Observations and Coaching
>
> Peer observers and coaches offer invaluable tools for improving teaching and learning and offer the opportunity to
>
> - Problem solve an instructional issue.
> - Analyze an aspect of teaching or instruction for the teacher's reflection.
> - Learn new ideas to try in the classroom.
> - Share classroom management techniques.
> - Apply a new teaching or instructional approach with immediate feedback.
> - Act as another set of eyes and report on an agreed-upon area of observation.
> - Demonstrate teaching to learn a new teaching or learning strategy from a colleague.
> - See expert or model coaching on a specific technique.
>
> _____
>
> Adapted from material from Research for Better Teaching, Inc., Acton, MA; and *Opening Doors: An Introduction to Peer Coaching* (Wolfe & Robbins, 1989).

1st and 2nd grade colleagues were telling me was not enough to prepare the children for the knowledge and skills they would need to learn in 1st grade. Then, one day, I had an epiphany! I was an observer in my own classroom, watching a teacher model a reading activity to support problem solving. I was incredulous that the children not only actively participated in the reading tasks, but they kept saying that they wanted to read more! I can't tell you how I felt. I believed that I was providing a developmentally appropriate classroom, and here were my students telling me what developmentally appropriate literacy learning was really about. I never looked back. The next day I began a peer coaching relationship that has revitalized my practice and helped me to set high-quality goals in literacy learning. I really have become part of our primary literacy and learning team. It's really true: "Out of the mouths of babes."

Choosing a Colleague for Peer Coaching

Teachers need to feel in control of their learning, including the learning that takes place in peer coaching. Therefore, assigning and pairing

---

FIGURE 4.5
Choosing a Peer Coach

When choosing a colleague for peer coaching, you may wish to consider the following:

- Would I or do I trust this person?
- Can I and do I want to build a professional relationship with this person?
- Do we both have a willingness to look at our teaching practices?
- Are we both willing to take risks, expose ourselves to mistakes, and learn from them?
- Are we both willing to find time in our already filled days to devote to peer coaching?
- Are we both willing to learn and apply the coaching process with integrity?

---

teachers dooms the peer coaching process. Assigned pairs of colleagues tend to go through the motions of peer coaching without receiving the full benefits. Discussing the value of peer coaching and providing opportunities for peer collaboration enables teachers to feel some control, in this case by selecting a partner. Figure 4.5 offers a list of considerations for choosing a colleague for peer coaching.

Improving student learning necessitates that teachers look not only at how and what they teach, but also at how they know students are learning. Therefore, reflecting on practice is critical. To this end, it is helpful to use an inquiry process. Routman (2000, p. 464) clearly describes the inquiry process. A teacher must wonder about something in order to develop a question that leads to an investigation. During the investigation, various perspectives and contrary ideas are considered, and data is collected and analyzed before the teacher reaches a new understanding. Then, at some later time, the inquiry process most likely begins again with a new "I wonder" question. The following is a menu of possible areas of inquiry for teachers to consider as they learn about and refine standards-based practices.

- Sharing feedback on minilessons that focus on learning strategies
- Using think alouds in minilesson demonstrations

- Planning and implementing standards-based lessons, routines, or units
- Creating a learning-centered classroom
- Managing a learning-centered classroom
- Creating and implementing high-quality classroom-based assessments
- Creating and implementing high-quality performance-based assessments
- Using data for teacher decision making
- Crafting student self-assessments
- Improving content instruction and student learning
- Using technology in the classroom

It is not enough for a school to suggest that staff use peer coaching; the school must provide training and support for the collaboration. If peer coaching is valued as a way to improve practice, the school needs to offer high-quality professional development, allocate the funds, and allow time for follow-up sessions. Consider the elements of quality provided in Figure 4.6 when designing professional development for peer coaching.

Once the appropriate professional development is in place to guide staff toward peer coaching, you'll need to focus on planning. Planning enables the peer coach to have clear goals for data collection during the observation of the teaching demonstration. The planning cycle includes a pre-observation meeting to discuss the needs of the teacher and students and to agree on specific data the coach will gather during the teacher demonstration. The teacher selects or designs a data-collection system and acts as a coach. Next, the coach observes the lesson using the observation system agreed on in the pre-observation meeting. The coach analyzes observation data and determines the best way to share information with the teacher. The post-observation meeting is for the peer coaching team to interpret the data and set a refinement or improvement goal, which can form the basis for another coaching cycle. Lastly, the team members reflect on the experience and give feedback to each other about the process. It is important to continue the peer coaching relationship for a least two rounds (two sets of observation for each teacher) to support improvement or refinement goals. Peer coaching requires

---

FIGURE 4.6

Professional Development for Effective Peer Coaching

Consider these elements of quality when choosing professional development in peer coaching:

- Trainer has experience and uses simulations, videos, demonstrations, and modeling to convey techniques, processes, and strategies.

- Training provides initial days to learn concepts and processes with at least 3 follow-up opportunities throughout the year, preferably half days or no less than 2 hours each, in order to debrief and process experiences being practiced in the school.

- Training components include a structured process for peer coaching, and numerous simulations and practice with reflective processing in the following skills:
  - Listening without judgment
  - Giving and receiving feedback
  - Questioning techniques
  - Using data collection techniques to focus observations
  - Working with conflict
  - Working with different learning styles
  - Knowledge of a developmental approach to adult learning
  - Using the peer coaching cycle

Adapted with permission from Garmston (1987); Leggett & Hoyle (1987); and Robbins (1991).

---

that the peer coach and the teacher reverse roles to benefit the teaching and learning in both classrooms. Figure 4.7 outlines a five-step procedure for peer coaching interactions.

Peer coaching was found to be vital if implementation of a new instructional practice was to be incorporated into the teaching repertoire. Teachers who had a coaching relationship were able to maintain new teaching strategies and use new teaching models appropriately compared with their teaching counterparts who tried to implement in isolation (Baker & Showers, 1982).

Learning data collection techniques is essential for maintaining a focus and enabling the person being coached to reflect upon and evaluate the data. A basic technique is script taping or scripting (Acheson & Gall, 1997). In

FIGURE 4.7
Five-Phase Coaching Model

This coaching model is effective with peer coaches or coaches working with beginning teachers. We recommend two full rounds of coaching to assist and to support change.

Phase	Description	Sample Coach Notes
Pre-Observation Conference*	Discuss standards and evidence, student strengths and weaknesses, classroom management, instructional strategies, and student assessment strategies of an upcoming lesson (e.g., teaching and learning activity or routine).	**Suggested prompt for getting the conversation started:** What are you concerned about that might help you improve your practice?
	Discuss the teacher's concerns or interests.	This first-year high school mathematics teacher is very concerned about one of her classes. She is discouraged about teaching because of this particular class, although her other classes are going well. She asked me to observe the class and to take notes during the whole 50 minutes. Together we decided that I will observe the behaviors of all students and use codes to denote their on-task behavior (T), off-task behavior (O), and disruptiveness (D).
	Teacher and coach agree that the coach will gather data on specific student or teacher behaviors during the observation. They also select or design a data-collection system.	I will observe 16 students. I will watch each student for about 1 minute. After I observe each student for 1 minute, I will repeat the process. We calculated that I will observe each student for a total of 7 minutes.

FIGURE 4.7 (continued)

Phase	Description	Sample Coach Notes
Classroom Observation	Coach observes lesson using observation system agreed on in the pre-observation conference. The coach collects only the agreed-upon data.	(excerpt from observation) Ray T T T O O T T T T T T O O T T Denise O O O O T T T T T T T T T T T T Charles T T T T T T T O O T T T T T T Ed O O O D D D D D T T T T T T D D Sue T T T T T O O T T T T O O T T Marjorie T T T D D D D T T T T T T D D

Analysis and Strategy	Coach analyzes observation data and determines best way to report to teacher.
	
	Coach determines interpersonal approach to use for the post-observation conference.
	
	Interpersonal Skills (Glickman, 1990)
	
	    Nondirective approach—coach uses listening, paraphrasing, clarifying and reflecting behaviors.
	
	    Collaborative approach—coach does more presenting, problem solving, and negotiating.
	
	    Directive (informational) approach—coach emphasizes directing and standardizing, giving teacher considerable information and restricted choice.
		Using Excel, I made a chart revealing what percentage of the time each student was on task, off task, or disruptive.
		
		Using a nondirective approach, I asked the teacher to look at the chart and see what she noticed. To her astonishment, she found that the students were on task more of the time than she thought.
		
		I also recorded who was disruptive and who else was involved. I asked her what she noticed about this data.

(figure continues on next page)

FIGURE 4.7 (continued)

Phase	Description	Sample Coach Notes
Post-Observation Conference	Coach shares data; together the coach and teacher interpret data. Teacher may choose an instructional improvement goal. The post-observation conference may change into a pre-observation discussion so that the coach and teacher can agree on a new observation and data collection effort for planned instructional changes.	I asked how she might like to use the data. She said that she would like to share it with her students and relate it to their grades. She said that she felt so relieved to see that the students were on task for much more of the time than she imagined and to find that she had placed the students who tended to be off task in the front of the room where she could see them.
Post-Analysis Conference	Coach collects and analyzes data about his coaching. Coach receives oral feedback from the teacher on coach's performance.	**Prompt:** Did this observation work for you? What suggestions do you have for refining it? The teacher found the charted data and bar graphs extremely useful and was astonished how much data could be collected on each learner. We will meet again after she crafts and executes a lesson using the data with the students.

*Five phases adapted from Gordon (1991).

this data collection procedure, the observer writes down what is seen and heard during a teaching demonstration. The purpose of this technique is for the observer to act like a mirror providing the teacher with data for reflection. Often teachers new to this procedure find it cumbersome. Allowing teachers to have numerous practice simulations is helpful. Here are some helpful hints for scripting:

- Use partial words.
- Note time every two minutes. If you forget something, the time note might jog your memory.
- Do not judge, just write what you hear.
- If you get muddled, stop, focus, note time, and start again.
- Don't write a continuous script. Write every 2 minutes.

Selective Verbatim (Acheson & Gall, 1997) is a type of scripting that is more focused. The observer records what is said, focusing on a type of concern chosen by the teacher. Focus areas might include

- Teacher questions
- Teacher responses to student questions
- Teacher directions or assignments
- General talk patterns
- Teacher control of student behavior
- Student responses to teacher questions
- Student-generated questions

Verbal flowchart (Acheson & Gall, 1997), another type of data collection, helps the teacher demonstrate how he responds both verbally and physically to students. Verbal flowcharts can help to determine how classroom procedures inhibit, encourage, or allow student participation. The observer draws a diagram of the class and creates a key with symbols to chart such things as who is contributing, who is questioning, and who does more of the talking. The focus and keys to be developed are as vast as the questions teachers seek to answer.

Charting on-task behavior is a data collection technique that allows a teacher to receive a record of academic behaviors for her analysis during instructional conferencing (Acheson & Gall, 1997). It requires the use of a seating chart to record academic behavior of students. The observer must know the teacher's expectations for the observation and create a legend for behaviors being observed. The types of behaviors often noted include such things as students being on task, distracted, off task, or nonproductive.

It is important to practice data collection techniques in simulations in order to develop some comfort with the tools and receive feedback regarding techniques, skills, and concerns prior to use with a colleague. Teacher pairs can develop additional data collection formats once they understand the principles behind data collection.

Using the right communication approach to share observation data enables teachers to effectively use the data. Glickman (1990) devised an interpersonal skills framework for giving feedback based on the developmental level of the teacher. He defined these approaches across a developmental continuum. Three of these approaches are appropriate for coaching purposes: (1) directive informational, (2) collaborative, and (3) nondirective.

Directive informational: Coach gives one or sometimes two possible options to solve the problem. This is a useful approach to use when working with novice teachers who lack experience.

A novice teacher is frustrated that her students have difficulty comprehending nonfiction texts. They don't seem to understand the information. The teacher reads the text aloud or chooses one student to read and the rest of the class listens. The coach asks the teacher who is doing most of the work. The teacher replies that she is, but doesn't know what else to do. The coach offers an effective reading comprehension strategy—using small sticky notes to code the text. Coding includes symbols such as I for interesting, BK for background knowledge, and TS for text-to-self connection. The coach says to the teacher that using this approach will set purpose for the students as well as keep them active as they read. The novice teacher would like to try the approach, but would like to see a demonstration. The coach agrees to demonstrate.

Collaborative: Together teachers share ideas and brainstorm to devise a solution to a problem or issue. Both teachers pool ideas to come up with the best solution.

A teacher talks to a colleague about the difficulty of finding independent reading books for a group of learners. The problem is that there aren't enough books in her classroom and she can't order any more this year. The colleague offers to loan a few books at the right reading level, but that won't be enough. The colleague also says that there are books in a closet that that no one is using, but that the books need to be assigned reading levels. Although there are resource books to guide in selecting the levels of those books, the teacher feels that this would be a large task to take on by herself. They agree to work together to assign levels to the books and to share them among their classes; they plan to devote a half-day of work time to the project during a teacher workday.

Nondirective: The colleague or coach listens to the teacher and acts like a mirror, using reflective questions for the teacher to respond to so that the teacher can generate solutions on her own.

A teacher shares with a colleague her disappointment with the results of a lesson on current events. The colleague asks for clarification by saying "Can you talk more about that?" and "What do you want to happen?" The teacher tells her colleague that she asked her students to read the article and to be ready to share their thoughts in a discussion. Now, she realizes that students need more support for reading nonfiction. The colleague then asks the teacher how else she could approach the problem. The teacher responds that she needs to model how students can mark up text to gain meaning and thinks that she can do a think aloud with the same piece to demonstrate how the students can interact with the text as they read. The colleague asks how the teacher thinks this lesson might go. The teacher responds that she believes she will see an improvement in their reading comprehension.

COGNITIVE COACHING

Cognitive Coaching is an essential component of leadership coaching and peer coaching. This original work of Art Costa and Robert Garmston is built from research on thinking skills, clinical supervision, and developmental supervision. Here are key assumptions of this work:

- All teachers and administrators can continually develop their intellect (recognition of untapped potential),
- Teaching performance is based on decision-making skills, and
- An enlightened colleague can significantly affect a teacher's cognitive processes.

Costa and Garmston (2002) think of coaching in terms of assisting in the movement of someone's beliefs, values, actions, and goals toward a new direction. The cognitive coach relies on the use of Socratic dialogue and insightful questions to enable the teacher to reflect and make decisions. Coaches use probing questions and paraphrasing techniques to elicit solutions to problem. Other key Cognitive Coaching skills include use of nonjudgmental responses, probing for specificity and precision in responses, paraphrasing, and wait time. Key dispositions of cognitive coaches are their abilities to be tentative and to trust that people have inner resources to achieve excellence. The cognitive coach serves as a mediator to assist the teacher in reflecting on practices and actions. The training includes tools for the following (Center for Cognitive Coaching, 2000):

- Maintaining rapport—interpersonal skills, body awareness
- Using meditative questioning—reflective questioning techniques that help teachers find solutions to their own problems and issues
- Exhibiting response behaviors—use of wait time, body language, paraphrasing, and clarifying by coach
- Pacing and leading—flow of interaction to allow thinking and responding, goal setting, and action orchestrated by the coach

A planning protocol is used as a post meeting in which the coach supports teacher reflection on practice. Outlined in Figure 4.8 is an example of the type of interactions that occur during the process of Cognitive Coaching.

TIME AND STRUCTURES

To make coaching a reality, much more than funding is needed to support initial professional development. Applying peer coaching in the everyday world of teaching, not just in simulations during training, facilitates shifts in teacher practice and ultimately in student learning.

Without thoughtful planning by leaders or leadership teams, coaching will not take hold, and the promise of moving toward collaborative reflection will become nothing more than empty rhetoric. Unfortunately, many teachers do not consider peer coaching because the structures needed to support teachers are nonexistent.

Effective planning prior to initial professional development experiences ensures successful collaborative learning relationships. Keep in mind Joyce

---

FIGURE 4.8
Cognitive Coaching

These are the elements of Cognitive Coaching that are used in preconferences and post-conferences. After each set of elements is an example of dialogue between the coach and the teacher. How are these examples similar to or different from observation conferences you have had, either as a coach or as the teacher being observed?

Questioning Elements of the Preconference (10 minutes or less)

1. Coach asks the teacher to elaborate on his learning goals and how he will know if students are learning during the lesson: "What cues will you have from students that they are learning during the lesson?"

2. Coach asks about the plans or strategies for reaching the objectives of the lesson.

3. Coach asks what she can pay attention to that will support the teacher's growth. What data would the teacher like the coach to collect? For example, proximity, direction giving, and effect of teacher moves on student performance.

Coach: Can you tell me what your learning goals are?

Teacher: I have started a unit on inferencing, because this is an area that needs strengthening.

Coach: Can you share with me what you have already done?

Teacher: I modeled the inferencing process using think alouds with pictures and with poems. I want to give the students a variety of opportunities to practice inferencing.

Coach: What are your plans for helping students infer in this lesson?

Teacher: I have modeled how to infer with two different sets of material. Now, in this next lesson I will review with them the tools they need to think about when inferencing. This time I will give them a very short story. I would like you to make sure that the words I am using are simple and clear. I don't want to lose them in the explanation.

Coach: I'm not quite clear what feedback you would like from me. Can you speak a little more about what you want.

Teacher: I think that I would like you to focus on the student discussions in small groups as they work together to delve deeply into the meaning of the short piece. I think that it is important to see if students are engaged, responding, and sharing their ideas. Yes, I would like you to note the level of engagement.

Coach: What does that mean to you?

Teacher: I've modeled and they've practiced how to effectively engage in lively discussions. I have given them feedback on their discussions several times. But, I know that they need more support. My goal is to have them move away from just round-robin answers in their group—which, by the way, they thought was discussion. I now want them to give evidence from the text, share their ideas, and engage and respond in constructive dialogue to extend their understanding. I am giving students many opportunities to demonstrate their understanding of what an inference is. I would like you to observe and record their responses.

(figure continues on next page)

FIGURE 4.8 (continued)

Coach: So, I will develop a code to try to capture those two things in each small group? Evidence from the text, and engagement in constructive dialogue.

Teacher: Yes, that would be helpful to me. And could you capture some of the dialogue? I would like to be able to listen to their conversations.

Coach: Okay, I'll record pieces of their conversations as well as use the code. And how many groups?

Teacher: There will be four discussion groups.

Questioning Elements of the Postconference

1. Using Socratic dialogue, the coach asks a question such as "How do you feel the lesson went?" Or "What are you recalling in the lesson that's leading you to those inferences?"

2. To develop self-coaching so that teachers can recall accurate details of what happened in the lesson, the coach asks, "How did what happened in the lesson compare with what you wanted?" Or "What might you have done differently?"

3. Finally, the coach might ask the teacher to apply new insights: "How will you use these insights in future lessons or in other aspects of your work?"

Coach: Here is the data from my observation of the small groups. What do you notice? How do you think the lesson went?

Teacher: Well, as I look at the data, I see that three out of the four groups were engaged and that they were using constructive dialogue. From your notes, I see that many students are now finding evidence from the text to support their inferences. Discussion and engagement are occurring more often than just a few weeks ago. I see that you were able to observe each group for five minutes.

Coach: What did happen in the lesson compared with what you wanted?

Teacher: I'm pleased with the level of conversation and I believe that my modeling, demonstrations, instructions, and repeated examples have paid off for about 85 percent of the class. Now this one small group performed as I expected—not that engaged.

Coach: What might you have done differently?

Teacher: I'm going to mix them up. I think that those three students need to work with other students. Putting them together just because of their reading level doesn't work.

Coach: How will you use these insights in future lessons or in other aspects of your work?

Teacher: I need to reconfigure the groups so that these three kids can work and talk to other students and see how other students engage in dialogue. Also, I need to do some more mini-lessons with some of the students so that they can continue to refine their discussions.

Coaches focus the relationship on trust and rapport, which enables teachers to be able to reflect on their teaching.

Adapted with permission from Sparks, D. (1990). "Cognitive coaching: An interview with Robert Garmston," *Journal of Staff Development, 11*(2), 12–15.

FIGURE 4.9
Planning List for Supporting Peer Coaching

General questions to spark thought	Please give specific answers
Is there weekly time built into peer coaching for the specific participating team?	When?
Are there opportunities for colleagues to communicate electronically?	Is our network up and running?
Does each colleague have access to a working computer during the day?	Where? When?
Is there space, such as a team planning room, where collaborations and discussions about education can occur?	Where will they meet?
Is there sanctioned release time during school when colleagues can work together or observe each other?	Will substitutes be needed? Is there money to pay them?
Are policies and procedures in place to support learning communities? Is there specificity in the documents regarding meeting time during the school day, remuneration, and value in teacher collaboration to improve teaching and student learning?	What policies and procedures? Are they in draft form? When will they be approved by the board?

and Showers' (1987) research on the implementation of professional development: When theory, demonstration, practice, and feedback are evident during the initial training in a new set of skills, 25 percent of teachers will transfer a new skill into practice, whereas 90 percent of teachers will transfer a new skill into their practice with theory, demonstration, practice, feedback, and coaching. So, even initial peer coaching training must be followed by coaching support during implementation.

Having a plan for the implementation of peer coaching is important. Plans must be made so that time is available to allow teachers to meet. Ensuring that there is a private place for interactions to take place is also necessary. Consider what policies and procedures need to be in place to support coaching relationships and environments. Figure 4.9 provides a planning list for supporting peer coaching.

Coaching encourages collaboration among colleagues, but it does not necessarily provide the opportunity for many or all members of the faculty to be engaged in collegial learning. Colleague support must be developed as a comprehensive system within schools and across the district, as is discussed in Chapter 5.

5

LEADING AND SUPPORTING COLLABORATION

THE FOCUS OF THIS CHAPTER IS ON THE SKILLS LEADERS NEED TO GUIDE A school or district in the implementation of a comprehensive colleague support system. These essential skills can be applied by individuals in any leadership position, including principals, central office staff, department chairs, and team leaders. These skills provide a common context for building systems and structures for the success of those teaching and learning within the system.

Although these skills are essential, they alone do not make a leader. Picture a leader who has mastered all the skills of leadership, but has no vision, does not empower others, and creates no excitement about the challenges at hand. The skillful leader without spirit builds capacity, but not commitment; the spirited leader with limited skills inspires, but does not deliver.

School leadership centers on structure and function. In the early 1980s, research into effective schools (Bates & Wilson, 1989) led to the unsurprising conclusion that many effective schools have effective principals. This finding led to the popular concept of the principal as superhero. Many schools, grasping this straw as they had countless others, attempted to locate such a principal, tried to mold one from the principal they already had, or lamented the fact that they couldn't expect to succeed without their own superhero.

Many years and thousands of burned-out principals later, we recognize that leadership for schools is about structure and function, not position (Glickman, 1997). Yes, a school may succeed with a skilled, charismatic principal. Equally inspirational and competent leadership, however, may come from the teaching ranks, the central office, the school board, parents, or the business community. Schools and districts are best able to sustain success when leadership is shared among these groups and focused on the primary functions of building commitment to the purposes of the organization.

When the purpose of the school is focused on implementing a comprehensive colleague support system, what leadership strategies will build shared commitment to this goal?

PLANNING FOR SUCCESS

In his groundbreaking work on creativity and leadership, Robert Fritz (1999) developed a structural tension charting process that enables a school or district to define its overriding goals and to define its current reality. The steps in the structural tension charting process are (1) setting goals, (2) defining current reality, (3) action planning, and (4) phasing. When applied to colleague support, the structural tension charting process can establish a path of least resistance within which we can create action plans, establish due dates and accountability, evaluate results, and adjust future actions.

Step 1—Setting Goals

Picture a school that decides to implement a colleague support system. There are two possible perspectives from which to set goals:

1. Set goals from a problem-solving perspective: Let's fix our teachers by having the strong ones support the weak ones, or the experienced ones support the inexperienced ones.

2. Set goals from a creative perspective: By the X school year, we will create a learning community in which all educators learn to support and learn from one another so that they can create high-quality teaching and learning experiences for all students.

What makes the second statement a good goal statement? It specifies a time frame (the school year); it names a product (a learning community); it operationally defines the product (in which all educators learn to support and learn from one another); and it states the purpose (high-quality teaching and learning experiences for all students).

Schools, like other organizations, flow in the direction of their goals. If the goal is to fix the young or less successful teachers, several things may happen:

• The goal is seen as belonging only to those teachers identified for the process by contract, policy, or procedure. Therefore, getting out of the process is a growth goal.

• The unit of change is seen as young, or less successful, teachers, rather than all educators.

• Poor or novice practice, rather than learning excellence, becomes the focus of intervention.

• The program narrows to focus on relatively few aspects of the complex learning process—often only organization and management.

• Effects on individuals in the system may increase initially, then level off or decline.

If, however, the goal is creating a supportive learning environment for adults that will lead to optimal learning experiences for students, here is what can happen:

• Responsibility for the goal is shared among all educators and all learners.

• Multiple measures are used to define success.

• Structures and strategies supporting the system are inclusive, not exclusive, retaining a broad scope within which growth can occur.

• Success, as defined by a variety of measures, for more teachers and more students because of the broad focus over time.

When this schoolwide approach was used in a Vermont middle school, the number of 8th graders meeting or exceeding standards in math problem solving jumped from 37 percent to 64 percent in one year.

Leadership Skills for Goal Setting. Advocate for goals that create what you want as an organization, such as increased proficiency in problem solving, rather than goals that address a problem, such as low test scores.

Principals and superintendents can establish such goals in a top-down design (this is what the principal of the Vermont middle school did), or teacher leaders or other staff members may propose goals. In any case, leaders need to leverage and allocate resources to support these goals and encourage and build advocates for the goals within the school and district. In the middle school, math teachers and some science and social studies teachers became early advocates for focusing on problem solving. As these teachers collaborated within their middle school team structures, certain teams emerged as vocal advocates. By midyear, most teachers and support specialists were actively supporting the goal of improving problem solving and supporting one another in attaining it.

Another key leadership skill related to goal setting is insisting on clarity. When will the goal be achieved? How will we know? As goals emerge, leaders initiate critical analysis. What results will we see in our school when we have reached this goal? If we see these results, will we agree that the goal is achieved? What will be our concrete measures of success? What performance indicators and performance measures will we establish? By continually asking these questions, and refusing to accept goals until the questions can be answered, leaders can create optimal conditions for goal monitoring. It is hard to harness energy to flow to a fuzzy goal.

Step 2—Defining Current Reality

Likewise, there are two reasons why it is hard to move from a fuzzy understanding of current reality: (1) we may not seek hard data, such as test scores, or ignore this data when it doesn't match what we want to hear; and (2) schools create structural tension that is too narrow in focus and cannot be easily measured. If a school defines its goal in terms of creating a school filled with excellent teachers, but defines its current reality only in terms of a narrow observation checklist, the narrowness of the reality definition will set the real goal as getting the checks in the right column.

Leaders must ensure that the statement of current reality aligns with the goal. Consider the goal in our example: By the X school year, we will create a learning community in which all educators learn to support and to learn from one another so that they can create high-quality teaching and learning experiences for all students.

FIGURE 5.1
Determining Current Reality

To determine your school's current reality, consider the following questions and seek these and other sources for pertinent answers.

Questions	Sources
How is colleague support, such as the teacher evaluation process, relicensure, professional growth plans, and tenure decisions, built into our current structures?	Documents, policies, and procedures Staff interviews
How much colleague support, and what types of support, do our teachers actually give?	Teacher interviews Review of teacher portfolios
Are there equity differences in the opportunity to learn from one another (e.g., do new teachers, struggling teachers, or teachers in certain departments, teams, or grade levels participate more than others)?	Teacher interviews Review of professional growth plans Review of teacher portfolios
How well do our teachers support one another? How do we know?	Teacher interviews Professional growth plans Teacher portfolios
How much professional development have our teachers had to support implementation of a colleague support system?	Review of professional development offerings and professional growth plans Teacher interviews
How well do the schedule, contract, and other structures support implementation of a colleague support program?	Schedule Contracts Teacher and principal interviews

What do we need to know about current reality? Figure 5.1 shows questions to ask and places to look for answers.

Be ruthless in defining your current reality! If something isn't working, say so. Identify gaps in implementation as well as areas that suffer from lack of support, either active or passive. Whenever possible, use statistics and specific qualitative data. If you don't put it on the table, it probably won't get resolved.

At the same time, be equally clear and specific in defining your assets and your support structures. These form the foundation of your action plan, and you don't want to sell yourself short.

Notice that the questions asked and data collected reflect every facet of our goal: high quality, all teachers, and realistic opportunities to succeed. We are considering the work produced, the conditions under which it is produced, and the opinions of those involved in producing it.

In defining current reality, the leader is vigilant so that important goals are not reduced to cursory definition. By insisting on critical analysis at this stage, she lays the groundwork for data-driven inquiry throughout the action planning process. Indeed, she builds the concept of inquiry as leadership.

Step 3—Action Planning: Creating the Implementation Plan

Once the goal is clear and current reality is defined, leadership focuses on action planning. Action planning defines concrete steps that can lead to achievement of the goal. Each step, in turn, becomes a goal in its own structural tension chart. This process, known as *telescoping* (Fritz, 1999), creates the implementation plan for the school.

Let's apply the process of telescoping to the example in the structural tension chart. Figure 5.2 shows the goal statement, an action plan that lists clear steps for proceeding, and a statement of current reality.

Leadership Skills for Action Planning. The leader has several roles in action planning. First, he must make certain that the proposed actions address the structural tension—that is, the energy flows from the current reality to the goal. Second, he must make certain that the actions, taken together, are likely to lead to the goal. Third, he must ensure that the actions are the right size—neither minute details nor sweeping generalizations. Each action should be specific enough to serve as a goal on a more detailed structural tension chart as the process of telescoping brings the process to the level of implementation, as shown in the example in Figure 5.3.

The leader can also help to make sense of the action plan by grouping actions into categories. In our example, the seven actions might be grouped

FIGURE 5.2
Sample Structural Tension Chart for Colleague Support

Goal: By the X school year, we will create a learning community in which all educators learn to support and learn from one another so that they can create high-quality teaching and learning experiences for all students

Action Plan:

Goal 1: Continue support of the district mentor training, with the goal of adding five newly trained mentors per year for the next three years. By year 3, ensure that all new teachers work in a mentoring relationship throughout the first two years of teaching, thus phasing out the supportive colleague model for new teachers.

Goal 2: Increase the number of teachers and administrators including colleague support in their professional growth plans to 60 percent in year 1, 80 percent in year 2, and 100 percent in year 3.

Goal 3: Increase the number of teachers and administrators including colleague support in the relicensure process to 60 percent in year 1, 80 percent in year 2, and 100 percent in year 3.

Goal 4: Create a professional development plan that includes opportunities to support all forms of colleague support, including live and electronic coursework, study groups, and opportunities to look together at student work, as well as mentor training. By year 3, all teachers and administrators will have participated in some form of professional development related to colleague support.

Goal 5: Continue the stipend for trained mentors.

Goal 6: Revise the schedule to provide for common unscheduled time for colleague support activities.

Goal 7: Devote three nonteaching days in the contract to colleague support activities.

Goal 8: Develop performance indicators and performance measures to track success in implementing this action plan.

Current Reality: Colleague support is built into the teacher evaluation process through the assignment of a "supportive colleague" to each new teacher. This colleague supports the new teacher for the first three months of the school year. Mentor training is available as an option. At present, seven teachers have completed mentor training. Teachers may

(figure continues on next page)

FIGURE 5.2 (continued)

build colleague support into their professional growth plans, either as a provider or receiver, at their discretion. Forty percent of teachers include some form of colleague support in their plans. Colleague support evidence may be submitted as part of the teacher portfolio for relicensure. In the past three years, 22 percent of teachers have included colleague support in the relicensure process. Neither the principal nor the assistant principal is involved in any form of colleague support at this time.

Teachers in the primary grades are much more likely to participate in colleague support. All kindergarten teachers, 60 percent of 1st grade teachers, and 50 percent of 2nd grade teachers now participate in colleague support.

The district continues its commitment to annual mentor training. There is no other formal professional development related to colleague support in the school or district. Other than the seven district-trained mentors in the school, only two other teachers have had formal training in colleague support, each in a previous assignment.

The contract includes a negotiated supplemental stipend for trained and practicing mentors. There are no other contractual provisions related to colleague support. There is no time in the schedule or the school calendar specifically earmarked for colleague support activities.

---

as incorporating existing offerings, developing new offerings, ensuring implementation, and evaluating success. These categories may be useful in assigning responsibility for monitoring implementation and evaluating results.

Step 4—Phasing: Building a Series of Steps for Implementation

Implementation sometimes fails because leaders try to implement everything at once. The tactic of phasing uses a series of steps for implementation, each building on the success of the previous steps. Phasing helps to build momentum and to make explicit the relationships among parts of the strategy at any time. By evaluating each phase as it evolves, leadership can make midcourse corrections, thus shaping implementation and increasing likelihood of success.

One might occasionally have the opportunity to open a new school, hire a whole faculty, and take a year for preplanning. That approach was taken by

FIGURE 5.3
An Example of Telescoping

Action Plan Goal 4: Create a professional development plan that includes opportunities to strengthen all forms of colleague support, including live and electronic coursework, study groups, and looking at student work, as well as mentor training. By year 3, all teachers and administrators will have participated in some form of professional development related to colleague support.

- Continue mentor training. Conduct a systems analysis to determine how mentor training interfaces with the overall professional development plan for colleague support.

- Work with the central office and local university to develop a 3-credit course in colleague support strategies. Make the course available by the fall of year 2.

- Develop a Web-based version of the course for implementation by the fall of year 3.

- Establish protocols and procedures for both whole faculty study groups (Murphy & Lick, 1998) and topic-driven study groups. Implement an initial whole faculty study group by the spring of year 1.

- Work with consultants and central office curriculum personnel to develop programs and procedures for looking at student work. Implement by spring of year 2.

- Discuss colleague support in the goal-setting process. Review professional growth plans to ensure that 100 percent of teachers and administrators have participated in some form of professional development related to colleague support by the end of year 3.

- Develop performance indicators and performance measures to evaluate the implementation of the professional development plan for colleague support.

Current Reality: The district continues its commitment to mentor training on an annual basis. There is no other formal professional development related to colleague support in the school or district. Other than the seven district-trained mentors in the school, only two other teachers have had formal training in colleague support, each in a previous assignment.

the Arizona Diamondbacks baseball team when they hired their manager a year before fielding a team and then won the 2001 World Series in only their fourth year of competition. Most of us, however, lead where we are, with whom we are working, amid the school year. Phase 1 involves improving the continuing activity while it is in process. In our example, teachers and administrators might carefully examine the mentoring training and program, the process of developing the professional growth plan, and the relicensing process, optimizing the time and structures already available for colleague support. The question is, are there ways in which we can better use what we have now? For example, can each professional be challenged to include at least one professional goal requiring colleague support?

Phase 2 involves developing new systems and procedures, yet the successful leader also pays special attention to management issues in this phase. Managing change in such areas as scheduling, budgeting, and supervision becomes even more important than it is while maintaining the status quo. Everyone is watching, just as they watch someone trying to get rich in a small town.

Besides being vigilant about operations management, leaders also become deeply involved in substantive changes in the work itself in phase 2. In this case, the learning and interactions of the adults in our system, and the genesis of the learning of our students, are under revision. Leadership demands range from developing and articulating changes in practice, to providing and participating in essential professional development, to ensuring that implementation is consistent and competent, to assessing and communicating results.

As new ways of working become the norm, and as results warrant their continuation, the challenges of Phase 3 involve sustainability and deeper involvement. Leaders must recruit new personnel who are willing and able to commit to a higher level of performance. Current staff must maintain momentum even as other initiatives demand time and attention. In phase 3, a key leadership attribute is stamina; leaders must stay the course if they expect others to do the same. As time progresses, some skills essential in phase 2, such as scheduling, become routine. Others, such as continuous assessment and communication of results and professional development for staff, must deepen over time. A successful phase 3 leader must be able to distinguish between the routine and the complex, and focus her energy and that of the organization on the latter without allowing the former to slip.

Leadership Skills for Phasing. Some leaders never succeed at all. Others succeed in phases 1 and 2, but lack the skills to sustain in phase 3 (this is one reason that turnover among school administrators is so high). Even the leaders who use structural tension planning for initial implementation may fail to adjust along the way.

Let's return to our example of colleague support. The school may successfully initiate changes in its current system in phase 1. Enthused by success, they revise and expand the program, change the schedule, provide professional development, and increase opportunities for colleague interaction. Both adult job satisfaction and student learning increase and the staff, administration, and community are happy with results in phase 2.

This school is now ready to enter phase 3. If leadership simply declares victory and moves on to the next project, over time it will have a trophy case of isolated projects. At such schools you'll hear "remember when we did colleague support (or cooperative learning, portfolios, or assertive discipline)?" In other words, the school is in a pattern of oscillation, changing as it moves along. Eventually, even the most charismatic leader has trouble generating enthusiasm for this nonproductive behavior.

Another trap is that the school might maintain the colleague support program at the same level long after the structural tension has been resolved, and the current reality has changed. This lack of attention leads to lassitude and, over time, saps the creative energy of the people in the organization.

Here is an example of how leadership focus may shift in the 3 phases of implementation of a colleague support system.

- Phase 1
    - Improving existing colleague support processes.
    - Working on research and development.
    - Developing design specifications.
    - Identifying performance indicators and performance measures
- Phase 2
    - Sharpening organizational and management strategies
    - Articulating expected changes in practice
    - Participating in professional development
    - Monitoring implementation
    - Assessing progress and communicating results

FIGURE 5.4

Divide and Think

- What is the end result we want?
- What is the current reality—*now*?
- What steps do we need to take to get to our end result?
- Are our actions working?
- What are we learning?
  - Is there another approach that might be better?
  - How do we know if we are on track?

Adapted from Fritz, R. (1999). *The path of least resistance for managers.* San Francisco: Barrett-Koehler. See also www.robertfritz.com.

- Phase 3
  - Staying the course
  - Redefining current reality and adjusting implementation accordingly
  - Sharing credit for success

Divide and Think (Fritz, 1999) is a technique that helps both leaders and the organization maintain focus. It is predicated on careful examination of the questions shown in Figure 5.4.

Leaders must be skillful at continually reframing successes within the construct of structural tension. In our example, the school might look at its success with colleague support and broaden the effort to include more people (e.g., paraprofessionals, volunteers, preservice teachers, and support staff); more strategies (such as internships and teacher exchange programs); or broader impact (such as district, statewide, or national leadership). The school would build upon the colleague support program, learning from the experiences in phases 1 and 2. Instead of a new project, the school moves an existing commitment to a more complex level of implementation. Using the Divide and Think strategy allows school leaders to fulfill the key leadership skill of maintaining the focus of the organization.

FIGURE 5.5
Catalytic Actions of Leadership

Critical Analysis   Facilitating

Advocating   Monitoring

Brokering

Source: Reprinted by permission of the Connecticut Academy for Education in Mathematics, Science & Technology, Inc., on behalf of the SSI States' supplemental grant from the NSF © 2001. This material is based upon work supported by the National Science Foundation under Grant No. ESR0092129. Any opinions, finding, and conclusions or recommendations expressed in this material are those of the authors and do not necessarily reflect the views of the National Science Foundation.

ACTIONS OF SUCCESSFUL LEADERS

The National Systemic Improvement Initiative (2001) has identified five catalytic actions by leaders that cut across contexts and components of leadership. Like catalysts in chemistry, these actions shown in Figure 5.5 can accelerate an action or lower the threshold at which the action may occur.

How can the five catalytic actions strengthen a colleague support system? Let's see how these catalytic actions play into our example and discussion.

Critical analysis involves initiating self-analysis of the school's or district's colleague support efforts and using critical friends and external evaluators. Critical analysis occurs at every step of structural tension. We analyze the goals for relevance, specificity, and rigor. We analyze current reality initially, and then again and again throughout each phase of implementation. Divide and Think is essentially an exercise in critical analysis.

The successful leader recognizes that analysis requires a combination of self-analysis, analysis by critical friends, and formal external evaluation. Each type of analysis needs to be built into the school's approach to structural tension. Questions to consider:

- What do research and best practice tell us about colleague support?
- How well are we supporting one another now?

Advocating is both advocating personally and ensuring internal and external advocacy. Like objects in nature, organizations experience inertia. Leaders need to advocate both for specific goals and for a structural approach to organizational development.

Leaders also must consciously identify and empower advocates, both within the school and within the community (including those in higher education and among policymakers). Building advocacy empowers others, builds leadership density, supports sustainability, and helps to dispel the myth of the superhero positional leaders. Questions to consider:

• How can I visibly support the colleague support strategy with the central office administration, board, and community?

• How do my day-to-day actions model colleague support in the school?

• Who, besides me, are key advocates? How can I maximize their impact on the system?

• How do I identify, build, and support new advocates along the way?

Brokering is obtaining, leveraging, and allocating resources. Resource development and deployment does much to build the credibility of leadership, both inside and outside the organization. Allocation of resources also speaks volumes about the real priorities of an organization and its leaders. Questions to consider:

• How can I support colleagues supporting colleagues through scheduling, budgeting, and other management areas?

• How can I identify and capture additional resources?

Facilitating involves enabling teamwork and collaboration. Skills in creating opportunities for collaboration; arranging schedules to optimize teamwork; and building structures and strategies for sharing, analyzing, and communicating results of collaboration are all key leadership skills. Questions to consider:

• How can I encourage teamwork and other forms of colleague support throughout the school?

• How can we set up systems for sharing our successes and learning from our failures?

• How can we best tell our colleague support story to the community?

Monitoring means ensuring reviews and feedback. Monitoring results and providing continuous feedback to all involved in school change are essential skills of leadership. By placing monitoring in the context of structural tension, leaders not only support goal-based diagnosis but also place it in a context in which it and the organization can and will succeed. Questions to consider:

- What are our key performance indicators and performance measures?
- How can we best measure the effects of short-term and long-term colleague support?
- How can we continue to use structural tension charting as a way to continue to evolve our colleague support program?

A comprehensive colleague support program requires strong, sustained leadership to build shared commitment and necessary assistance for those teaching and learning within the system. In this chapter, drawing on the work of Robert Fritz, we suggest a four-step process, including setting goals, defining current reality, action planning, and phasing. Tools and techniques, including structural tension charting, telescoping, and Divide and Think are introduced in support of leadership during program implementation. The chapter concludes with discussion of five catalytic actions identified by the National Systemic Improvement Initiatives that transcend all aspects of leadership. In the next chapter we will turn attention to leadership for building learning communities.

6

BUILDING AND SUSTAINING LEARNING COMMUNITIES

School leaders in all positions are simultaneously charged with two major responsibilities related to organizational development. First, they must lead both the staff and the instructional program to ensure the best possible education for all students. Second, they must manage people, resources, and infrastructure efficiently and humanely within a collaborative learning community.

Balancing these tasks requires a commitment to a formative process of professional growth that sustains the vitality and development of each adult in the learning community so that students are well served. For a school to function as a learning community, its members must share assumptions fundamental to professional growth. Froese (2002) suggests the set of assumptions in Figure 6.1.

BUILDING A LEARNING COMMUNITY

Examples from the research provide purpose and direction for building and sustaining learning communities. How, then, may these initiatives and practices be implemented? Refer to Figure 6.2 for a summary of the steps that are detailed in this chapter. They are practical steps that can guide development of a teaching and learning community and can be effectively

---

FIGURE 6.1

Fundamental Assumptions for Learning Communities

1. Each professional educator wishes to grow in effectiveness, confidence, and competence.

2. A supportive environment of peers, superordinates, and fellow staff induces formative process.

3. Reflective learning and professional growth require valid objective data and nonjudgmental feedback.

4. Organizational culture demonstrates these principles:
   - Effective learning for students is the goal.
   - People are regarded as able, valuable, and responsible; they are treated accordingly.
   - Fairness is essential to all processes.
   - Collaboration and mutual trust elicit confidence in formative process.

5. Growth planning is an introspective, reflective, self-initiated process.

_____

Adapted from Froese, E. E. (2002). "Professional growth programs." In Wideen, M., *The professional development dissortium*. Port of Spain: Ministry of Education of Trinidad and Tobago.

---

used at the school, cluster, or district level. The steps are iterative and are implemented most effectively as part of a continuous improvement cycle.

Policies, Procedures, and Contracts

Policies, procedures, and contracts are essential for an organization's well-being, and they create a foundation upon which to build trust. For example, a district may adopt a policy requiring a mentoring program for all teachers in the first three years of employment. If the district doesn't supply the foundation for the policy, trust between the district, the schools, and the staff will erode. To show support for the policy, the district can delineate the roles and responsibilities of mentors and mentees and establish expectations. For example, the Richland School District Two in

---

FIGURE 6.2

Steps to Building a Teaching and Learning Community

- Ensure that policies and procedures support collaboration
- Identify and support teacher leaders
- Create time for collaboration
- Redefine supervision and evaluation in a collaborative context
- Use data to plan for change
- Evaluate the teaching and learning community and its impact on students
- Tell your story

Columbia, South Carolina, has developed extensive procedures for mentors and mentees, a comprehensive teacher handbook, a checklist of quarterly expectations, and regular internal and external evaluation processes. Richland Two has cut the number of teachers leaving in the first three years to 12 percent, less than half the national average (Mellette & McCollum, 2005). In addition, the district needs to align the new policies with current and new staff contracts, which may stipulate compensation and release time. Careful analysis of existing policies, contracts, and procedures, as well as establishing criteria and filters for developing new ones are important steps in building a learning organization.

Policies are typically developed by state boards of education and local school boards or ministries of education, provincial authorities, or boards of trustees. In any case, policy development is a quasi-legislative process. Elected or appointed representatives draft policies, often in response to legislative requirements, requirements for accreditation, or community priorities. Well-crafted policies provide clear statements of intent, provide guidelines for action, and establish indicators of success. Policies are intended to last, and procedures for policy revision in public settings typically require one or more public notices of intent, opportunity for public input and discussion, and formal votes of the governing board.

Procedures establish structures and strategies for the implementation of policies. Procedures can exist at the district, school, unit (such as department team or grade level), and classroom levels. Effective procedures clearly communicate the parameters for implementation and provide explicit guidelines for educators, the community, parents, and children.

Contracts are negotiated agreements between organizations or individuals or both. Contracts provide deliverables and performance specifications for both parties and terms of agreement for compensation, delivery schedules, and contract administration.

Ideally, policies, procedures, and contracts are internally consistent and form a logical, seamless set of guidelines for the work of the school and district. In reality, even the best-intentioned policies, procedures, and contracts evolve over time; therefore, their provisions can become contradictory, redundant, or irrelevant.

> A new superintendent is committed to building learning organizations in her schools, and she has the support of her board in that endeavor. She finds that policies have proliferated over the years so that bureaucratic management takes inordinate amounts of time. Further, procedures are not explicitly linked to policies and are sometimes inconsistent with policy guidelines. Contract language is similarly overprescriptive, especially regarding the supervision and evaluation process. Although these issues are consistent across the various categories of policies, procedures, and contract language, the superintendent elects to begin with supervision, evaluation, and instruction.

How, then, are the steps for building a teaching and learning community, shown in Figure 6.2, implemented? Here are some concepts and examples.

Step 1: Establishing Intent. Given the new superintendent's scenario, the first step is to build consensus of intent. A clear statement of intent is found in Figure 6.3.

Formal adoption of the statement of intent by stakeholders, such as the school board, administrative council, and teachers' organization, is highly desirable. Sometimes, however, one or more of these groups will take a wait and see attitude. Even so, assuming sufficient support, move ahead with implementation. The analysis process that follows gives ample opportunity for building support.

Fritz (1999) argues that top-down leadership is appropriate and even essential at this step. In the scenario, the new superintendent has the support of the board and has the opportunity to champion the learning organization early in her tenure. Taking a visible, active lead role is critical to overcoming inertia.

FIGURE 6.3
Sample Statement of Intent

During the X school year, we will analyze our policies, procedures, and contract language so as to reach these outcomes:

- Expertise and resources will be shifted from bureaucratic management to improving teaching and learning.
- We will reduce the complexity and regulation of supervision and evaluation policies and procedures and increase opportunities for collaboration related to professional growth.
- We will ensure that our policies and procedures related to instructional practice are clear, coherent, and supportive of effective teaching.
- We will collaborate in ensuring that the contract language is clear, consistent, and fair to all parties.

We will do all of the above so that we can focus on improving instruction to enhance student learning.

Experienced school or district leaders, whether they are administrators, teachers, or board members, can likewise take definitive action in bringing this issue to the fore.

Step 2: Analysis. The purposes of analysis are (1) to begin developing a learning community, and (2) to recommend additions, deletions, or changes in policy and procedure based on the analysis. The analysis of policy and procedure is relatively nonthreatening (as opposed to analysis of instructional practice), produces concrete results, and moves forward relatively quickly. Early visible success in this arena lays the groundwork for potentially more difficult contract negotiations and the complexities of changing classroom practice.

> Having reached consensus on intent, the superintendent, teachers' organization, administrative council, and school board appoint representatives to an ad hoc policy analysis committee. The teacher's organization president, superintendent, and board chairperson serve ex officio.
>
> The committee engages an experienced policy analyst who guides it through the analysis of policies related to supervision, evaluation, and instruction. Following a thorough discussion of policy, the committee recommends policy changes to the board.

FIGURE 6.4
Policy Analysis Protocol

- What are the goals of the policy?
- What events led to the policy?
- What are the assumptions underlying the policy?
- What are the intended effects of the policy?
- What are potential unintended effects, both positive and negative?
- What are alternatives to the policy? What are plusses and minuses of each?
- What are recommendations related to the policy? What questions remain to be answered related to the policy?

Note: Depending on purpose or circumstance, the protocol may be employed to raise questions, generate recommendations, or both.

Source: Adapted from Vermont Policy Analysis Protocol by permission of Vermont Association for Supervision and Curriculum Development.

Policy analysis is complex, and finding a consultant to support the process may be warranted. An experienced policy analyst brings an outside perspective to the resources and obstacles in the school or district and may see connections that insiders miss. The independent analyst can also ask questions that are essential but awkward or even dangerous for insiders to raise. He may not slay the sacred cow, but neither does he have to accept her deity.

Whether or not an outside consultant is used, the ad hoc committee should adopt a protocol for policy analysis. An excellent protocol, developed by the Vermont affiliate of the Association for Supervision and Curriculum Development, is summarized in Figure 6.4.

Of special interest is the analysis of intended and unintended effects. Rarely is a policy adopted out of malice. It is important to recognize the good reasons for the policy's initial adoption and then to determine what unintended effects have unfolded. For example, a policy requiring that principals engage in at least three formal observations of each teacher annually probably had the intended effects of increasing the principal's role as instructional leader and bringing about consistency of practice. The time demands related to the policy's implementation might be so overwhelming that the observations are reduced to pro forma episodes accompanied by feedback through meaningless checklists. Reducing the number, varying the context, and increasing the quality of interactions may have greater impact on both professional growth and student learning.

Given that the goal is to improve student learning, the policy analysis process should evaluate each policy in relation to that goal. Fritz (1999) advocates use of what he calls *digital decision-making*. Digital decision making is a method of dividing a decision into structural components and assigning digital values to them. Then, a rigorous analysis is used to organize the components into a structural hierarchy. In this case, each policy should be assigned a plus (it supports increased student learning), a minus (it gets in the way of student learning), or a zero (it has little or no impact on student learning). This process should initially proceed individually and quickly; after a preliminary review of the policies, each person should individually rate each policy and then compare and tally results. Then the committee can discuss results and determine where consensus exists.

Using our scenario, consider the policies that support increased student learning as a group. Are these policies, as a group, sufficient for guiding development of procedures related to supervision, evaluation, and instruction? If not (and they probably are not), what additions from the "zero" group (as tallied) will complete the policy context? Can these be refocused to positively affect student learning?

Once these policies have been analyzed, the sufficiency question should be repeated. In this case, the group considers new policies that can be developed to complete the policy set.

The policy analysis committee has no authority to set policy. Therefore, its recommendations need to go to the governing body, usually the school board, through its policy subcommittee. Because the board endorsed the procedure to begin with, and because members were active in the process, it should be receptive to the recommendations of the committee. Nonetheless, the board will properly guard its obligation and authority to set policy and will fine-tune the recommendations, adding and deleting as it sees fit. The ad hoc committee should expect changes and work proactively during the policy adoption process. The result is almost always a leaner, less bureaucratic set of policies and marks the beginning of the critical process of building focus and trust in the learning community.

> Once the board completed the policy review, both the central administration and each school analyzed procedures. Their goal is to ensure that procedures effectively and efficiently implement policies and to delineate which procedures will be consistent across units and which will be locally determined. A districtwide ad hoc committee replicated the policy analysis. In this case, however, a second sorting process assigned procedures to the classroom, unit, school, or district level. The consultant worked with the districtwide ad hoc committee to develop a set of procedure review protocols and accompanying training materials. A set of training processes for school leadership teams followed.

Although the principle of aligning policy and procedure seems obvious, it is less common than one might think. A concerted, consistent review process at all levels of the organization is even more rare, but it is essential for these reasons:

1. A cluttered policy manual accompanied by irrelevant, obsolete procedures can breed cynicism and distrust.

2. The procedures have direct and immediate impact on teachers and students in the classroom and, therefore, have the greatest potential of impacting student learning.

3. Because procedure exists at the classroom, unit, school, and district levels, all educators have a direct stake in the procedure alignment process, and, therefore, this process has immediate effect on developing the learning organization at all levels.

> The consultant provided formative feedback throughout the policy review process. Once the process was complete, she completed a top-to-bottom review of policies and procedures for supervision, evaluation, and instruction to identify gaps, redundancies, and conflicts. Following a final revision process, the policies and procedures were distributed to all educators in print form, made available in school and public libraries, and posted on the district and school's Web sites for public reference and review.

Depending on the size and complexity of a district or school, the top-to-bottom analysis may be accomplished by in–house staff. In any case, it is a most important step and requires a skilled analyst to tighten the final product. This step will save work and frustration down the line.

> During the policy and procedure analysis processes, both the teachers' organization and the board noted places in which contract language did not align with emerging policies and procedures. In some cases, the two sides agreed that the language should be made consistent in the next round of contract talks. In other cases, one group or the other indicated that proposed policies or procedures were germane to contract language and would therefore need to be subject to negotiations. In all cases, the parties agreed that no policy or procedure directly in conflict with the contractual agreements in place would be implemented prior to contract revision.

Both the board and the teachers' organization have strong vested interests in their roles in developing fair, responsive contractual agreements. It is wise to move slowly and deliberately in contract revision, building trust along the way.

The policy and procedure review process described above is a proven strategy for building learning communities. Depending on the complexity of the school or district, this review may take a year or more; yet, it is worth the time and effort. It streamlines processes, builds trust, and focuses the agenda on student learning. Often the success of this approach is then replicated in policy areas such as budget, personnel, and safety.

During this process, other aspects of building learning communities are already in process. One of the most important is the identification and nurturing of teacher leaders.

IDENTIFYING AND SUPPORTING TEACHER LEADERS

Because student learning is the goal, and teachers are the most direct conduit between the student and learning, teacher leadership is essential in building a learning community. While specific aspects of teacher leadership have been discussed throughout this book and elsewhere, this section focuses on identifying teacher leaders and providing specific supports that can help them succeed.

The term "teacher leader" can be used in multiple contexts, from identifying the person who orders the spelling workbooks, to quasi-administrative functions, to those who serve in roles of colleague support as described in this book. In the sense that every adult in the school or district is a member of the teaching and learning community, all are teachers and all are teacher leaders. Nonetheless, it is important to identify key teachers who will learn specific skills, expand their knowledge, become part of the support systems, and can help to construct an empowered base for decision making (Martin, 2002).

You already know some potential teacher leaders. They may occupy roles of formal leadership, such as team leaders, department chairs, or association leaders. They may be the early adopters—the teachers who are first out of the gate on every innovation—or they may have received awards of excellence and National Board Certification. Although these recognized leaders are important, it is equally essential to identify new teacher leaders. Some places to look for new leaders are listed in Figure 6.5.

Identification, then, enhances leadership talents and capabilities already existing in the school and district and helps to ensure continuous nurturing of new leadership talent. The goal is to build shared and distributed leadership throughout the learning community. This leadership should be balanced as to role, experience, content expertise, and demographics. Leadership should include at least one direct connection for every adult in the organization.

Teacher leadership is a powerful feature of a learning organization, yet efforts to establish teacher leadership programs often fail. Here are common causes of failure:

• **Overcomplexity in defining the role.** Start focused and let additional leadership opportunities evolve over time. Identify finite and specific leadership expectations, such as serving as a mentor, analyzing policy, or serving on a site-based management council; acting in all those capacities may not be possible, at least at first.

• **Leaving the nature of the role undefined and poorly understood.** Make sure that there are specific deliverables and performance responsibilities for the teacher leader and communicate them to the leader and to all adults in the learning organization. Ambiguity breeds distrust.

• **Misuse or overuse.** There is a natural tendency to overdeploy our best resources. If you have defined the role, live within the definition. If it needs to expand or refocus, make sure that the teacher leader understands

FIGURE 6.5
Sources for New Teacher Leaders

Check the ranks of existing teacher leaders—department chairs, team leaders, or association officers.

Look to teachers of recognized excellence—National Board–certified teachers or those recognized by staff, community, or professional organizations as outstanding teachers.

Review individual professional development plans. Which teachers are pursuing leadership opportunities on their own? Which are engaged in collaborative learning opportunities? Which are in productive mentor relationships?

Identify emerging leaders in curriculum work, assessment development, and similar endeavors related to teaching and learning.

Seek new leaders in processes related to the learning organization, such as the policy and procedure review process, mentor training, and other forms of teacher support.

Ask. Many people never lead because they are never asked to. It is not enough to put out an "all-call." Specific invitations yield results. Be clear about what you are asking the teacher to consider doing, why, and how it is of direct benefit to her.

why and has a real opportunity to say no to the extra demands. Again, if responsibilities do expand, make sure that everyone knows it, not just that leader.

• **Lost opportunities.** A teacher leader who invests in additional training and devotes energy to a leadership responsibility wants the opportunity to perform. Although over use can lead to burnout, under-utilization of talents can lead the teacher leader to perceive that she is not valued. Don't get too busy to figure out productive ways to keep your leaders busy.

• **Lack of feedback.** As in any professional role, continuous growth is fostered by data-driven, objective feedback. The feedback should be directed to improved performance and should provide the teacher leader with information to reflect upon and to use in setting goals for her own professional growth.

Nancy Herman (author) recently worked with a group of teacher leaders who really did not know how to define their jobs. By creating their own action plan with products, they defined a doable job. The administrators were quite happy that the jobs finally became articulated and served as a point of refinement and negotiation between administrator and teacher leaders. Figure 6.6 includes practical suggestions for supporting teacher leaders.

FIGURE 6.6
Supporting Teacher Leaders

- Develop a written memorandum of understanding with each teacher leader specifying roles, deliverables, and expectations for support.

- Use the principles of colleague support included in this book. For example, ask the new teacher leader to select a mentor or supportive colleague.

- Develop generic teacher leadership professional development for all teacher leaders as well as specific development opportunities for each role. Do not expect the teacher leader to perform prior to the opportunity to learn. Don't assume that good people can wing it— although they may be able to do some of the job, it will not be within the parameters of the expectations in a learning organization.

- Provide regular opportunities for teacher leaders to interact and learn from one another.

- Provide specific data to each teacher leader on an ongoing basis. Schedule regular performance discussions.

- Continuously engage teacher leaders in identifying colleagues and planning for succession and maintenance within the program. A great mentor may not want to mentor forever, or every year. Involve the teacher leaders in building their own ranks.

- Build a graceful exit strategy into the teacher leadership system. The teacher leader should know that if circumstances change at home or at work, or if new leadership opportunities arise, there is a professional way to move on.

FINDING TIME FOR COLLABORATION

Beyond question, time is the most difficult variable to manage in a learning organization. Teaching is an intensive, consuming profession, and it is unreasonable and ultimately counterproductive to think that all time for collaboration can be found within existing schedules. It is equally unrealistic to think that no reallocation from current practice is possible and that new time must be found for everything. A balance between reallocation of time and investment of new time and ways of working can lead to a viable, collaborative learning organization.

Make no mistake; this is never easy. It requires a combination of political will, resource investment, personal self-sacrifice, and courage from all parties. As long as all parties recognize the need for sacrifice, and all are willing to give some, but not all, it is possible to find time for collaboration.

There is no single best solution to the time dilemma, and each district and school must address this issue in its own context. However, Figure 6.7 summarizes examples of strategies that have succeeded.

Having trouble finding time to work together? Examine your systems and current practices, set priorities, and eliminate what is not essential. Consider these potential sources of time:

• Look at your policies and procedures. If anything does not directly support student learning, consider whether it is essential or needs to occur as often as it does now.

• Review the supervision and evaluation process. Is the clinical supervision model the best use of time; does it need to occur as often for all teachers?

• Look within the assessment program. In a high school, can standards-based end-of-course assessments meet the needs for accountability both at the student and the school level, or do we need to test in April and again in May?

• Guard against the proliferation of curriculum. If there is a new state mandate for a curricular area, such as weapons education, do we add this to the already overloaded schedule or place it within existing curriculum, making sure that it fits logically with existing content and that something goes out as something goes in?

FIGURE 6.7

Finding Time for Collaboration

To find time for staff to collaborate, the school and district may need to consider creative arrangements that may affect some or all the following areas.

Supervision and evaluation process

Assessment program

Organization of the school day

Organization of the school year

Use of professional development time

Differentiating instructional patterns

Using support staff

Clerical use of technology

Collaborative use of technology

• Carefully review the school day and school year. Consider these questions:

○ Is there, or can there be, time in the day for collaboration?

○ Is there a need to add (and pay for) additional days in the year? If so, should these be student days or teacher days or both?

○ When should these extra days be scheduled and how will they be used for maximum effect on student learning?

○ Is time at the beginning and end of the day being used effectively? Should the school week be reconfigured?

One school reviewed their traditional hours, with the students leaving campus at 2:45, and the staff staying until 3:30 each day. They revamped the schedule so that students stayed until 3:15 each day, but didn't begin class until 10 a.m. on Wednesdays. The staff gained two hours of collaborative planning time weekly at a productive time of day, and students gained a half hour per week of instructional time.

• Carefully review use of time. If there are five professional days in the calendar, review how they are they being used. It is difficult to justify asking for five more days without compelling evidence that the existing days are being used to maximize collaboration and improve student learning.

• Consider whether differentiated instructional patterns can free up time. Although small class size ratios are essential for optimal student learning in many areas, determine whether there are aspects of the curriculum that lend themselves to large group instruction. Given professional development in large group techniques, and appropriate facilities, materials, and management support, students may learn as much or more of some content and skills in large groups, freeing up substantial time in the workday for collaboration.

• Use support staff and technology to relieve teachers of clerical and administrative chores, freeing them for collaboration. Even if only small amounts of time are spent in taking attendance, collecting milk money, and tracking down library books, each chore interrupts the focus on learning and fragments the school day. If these tasks can be delegated, automated, or both, collaborative activities are less likely to feel burdensome.

• Use technology to save substantial time in planning, record keeping, and communication. Can technology actually do this? The answer is an unequivocal yes, provided that the teacher has access to the hardware and software, adequate training in its use, and reasonable assurance that it is going to work.

• Use technology in the collaborative process itself. Again, given the caveats of access, training, and viability, learning communities can work effectively using strategies such as virtual learning campuses, interactive video, threaded discussions, and shared editing software. Technology does not preclude the need for personal interaction, but can supplement it in productive ways.

Time considerations are difficult. As with policy, time allocation decisions almost always were made for good reasons. The scheduling of time has evolved, and in every situation some individuals have investment in maintaining the status quo. Nevertheless, it is possible in almost any organization to use time more wisely. By keeping the goal of student learning at the forefront of the decision-making process and by ensuring that time changes actually do enhance collaborative practice, it is possible to make inroads into this most difficult dilemma.

Use Data to Build and Sustain the Learning Community

Much has been written elsewhere (e.g., Love, 2002; Carr & Harris, 2001) about the use of data related to student performance, learning opportunities for action planning, and overall school performance. How can data analysis be specifically applied to building and sustaining the learning community?

Performance Indicators and Performance Measures

It is useful at the outset to distinguish between performance indicators and performance measures. *Performance indicators* operationally define the principles—in other words, they provide a set of observable conditions, practices, and results that we agree represent the principles. It is neither necessary nor practical to identify every possible performance indicator for a principle. Rather, each staff member should agree on a finite set that he can remember and track.

Performance measures provide the means by which we track our progress in relation to each performance indicator. These measures can be qualitative, quantitative, or a combination of both. The word *measure*, in this case, is not restricted to numbers. Whether qualitative or quantitative, the measures need to be reliable and valid for their stated purpose of measuring the performance indicator. Figure 6.8 illustrates some possible performance indicators and performance measures for the principles included in Figure 6.1.

Effort and Impact

A key principle for data-driven learning communities is to move the focus from effort to impact. *Effort* is how much of something we do. *Impact* measures how much difference we are making. For example, if we want to measure the success of our math program, the emphasis should not be on the time spent in math class or the amount of professional development the teacher received, but rather on how well our students perform in mathematics.

Analyze the performance indicators and performance measures in Figure 6.8. You will note that effort measures still exist. Indeed, it is very important to continue to measure key effort indicators because the answers to increasing impact may well lie in this data. For example, staff members

FIGURE 6.8 Examples of Performance Indicators and Performance Measures		
Principle	Performance Indicators	Performance Measures
Effective learning for students is the goal.	Student performance on classroom assessments. Student performance on school and district assessments. Student performance on statewide and national assessments. Students' academic and career success after leaving the school.	Increased percentages of students meeting or exceeding standards or standards-based assessments at classroom, cluster, and school levels. Decreased disparity among student performances disaggregated by gender, ethnicity, income, and special needs. Improved student performance on nationally referenced examinations (such as college entry exams). Student and parent responses to follow-up surveys and interviews.
People are regarded as able, valuable, and responsible, and are treated accordingly.	All members of the learning community can describe their work in terms of the shared priorities of the learning community. Meetings and staff interactions include examination of open questions, inviting all staff to explore their ideas and reasoning. Tasks are established in a way that requires collaborative use of unique skills and talent sets from multiple participants.	Staff surveys and interviews, analyzed for key references to shared priorities. Review of meeting agendas and minutes; observations of actual meetings at various levels of the school organization. Task analysis, including analysis of individual contributions and group processes.
Fairness is essential to all processes.	All existing and newly proposed policies and procedures undergo a rigorous review for bias and fairness. Work plans, meeting agendas, and performance reviews include attention to fairness to all members of the learning community.	Policy and procedure analysis yields no instances of bias or unfairness. If such instances are identified, the policy or procedure is modified accordingly. Review of work plans, meeting agendas, and performance yields fewer instances of bias and unfairness over time.

	FIGURE 6.8 (continued)	
Principle	Performance Indicators	Performance Measures
Fairness (continued)	Meetings are conducted in a fair and open fashion at all levels of the school organization. Individuals and subgroups feel that they are treated fairly.	Process observers at all meetings monitor fairness, and fewer instances of unfair behavior are reported over time. Individuals report that they are being treated fairly in surveys and interviews. The number of formal grievances or other job actions decreases over time.
Collaboration and mutual trust elicit confidence in formative process.	Increased numbers of staff members participate in formative, collaborative processes. Staff members exhibit increased confidence in formative processes.	Analysis of staff members participating in formative process indicates increases in the number of different staff involved and the level of involvement. Staff members report increased confidence in formative process in surveys and interviews.

will not feel confident in the formative process if they never participate in such processes.

However, the emphasis should be on impact. Our bias is that in any learning community in a school, the primary impact analysis should tie to student learning. Hence, the first principle would be part of the equation in any learning organization. The others will evolve over time.

Finding Time to Collect and Use the Data

Data-driven decision making only works if you have the data to analyze. But where do you find the time to initiate an impact-focused data-driven culture in your learning community? Here are some suggestions:

Make your data serve multiple purposes. You are probably collecting student data for action planning and statewide accountability. Use this same data for student performance goals for your learning community, supplementing the data if necessary.

Use process observers. Garmston and Wellman (1999) have developed seven norms of collaborative work, shown in Figure 6.9. Figure 6.10 presents a form for assessing these norms.

At each schoolwide, staff, or department meeting, appoint a process observer to assess these norms and report out at the end of the meeting. Include a copy of the norms with each agenda. Over time, the use of process observers does four things:

1. It provides clear expectations for collaborative behavior.

2. It provides immediate feedback to the learning community.

3. It provides data for tracking collaborative behavior over time.

4. It empowers members as the role of process observer rotates among them.

Survey seldom and wisely. Never use six surveys when one will do. By determining and agreeing to your performance indicators, you establish the parameters for the performance measures that you need to assess (at least in part) by survey. Identify these measures in writing, and let staff members know that they will be given a survey related to these items in the year ahead. Always announce the survey timing well in advance and remind staff why this data is important. Focus your survey on the identified areas—resist the temptation to ask a question because "it would be nice to know." Survey construction deserves careful consideration, as the data is no better than the question that elicits it. Share the results with all staff in the context of your overall data analysis.

Interview few people, in depth. Surveys are excellent tools for getting an overall picture and for including all staff in data creation. Interviews provide opportunities to explore selected issues in greater depth and require a different level of investment and thought from both the interviewer and interviewee. It is much better to invest limited time in a few deeply engaging interviews than to attempt many superficial interviews. Again, prepare your questions carefully, tying them closely to the performance indicators you have set. Interviews also give you the opportunity to explore related issues or perspectives that you may not have considered. This opportunity is good, as long as you don't lose the focus on the topic at hand.

FIGURE 6.9
Norms of Collaborative Inquiry

Pausing
- Listens attentively to other ideas with mind and body
- Allows time for thought after asking a question or making a response
- Rewords in own mind what others are saying to further understand their communications
- Waits until others have finished before entering the conversation

Paraphrasing
- Uses paraphrases that acknowledge and clarify content and emotions
- Uses paraphrases that summarize and organize
- Uses paraphrases that shift a conversation to different levels of abstraction
- Uses nonverbal communication in paraphrasing

Probing
- Seeks agreement on what words mean
- Asks questions to clarify facts, ideas, stories
- Asks questions to clarify explanations, implications, consequences
- Asks questions to surface assumptions, points of view, beliefs, values

Putting Ideas on the Table and Pulling Them Off
- States intention of communication
- Reveals all relevant information
- Considers intended communication for relevance and appropriateness before speaking
- Provides facts, inferences, ideas, opinions, suggestions
- Explains reasons behind statements, questions, and actions
- Removes, or announces the modification of, own ideas, opinions, points of view

Paying Attention to Self and Others
- Maintains awareness of own thoughts and feelings while having them
- Maintains awareness of others' voice patterns, nonverbal communications, and use of physical space
- Maintains awareness of group's task, mood, and relevance of own and others contributions

Presuming Positive Intentions
- Advocates for own ideas and inquires into the ideas of others
- Acts to provide equitable opportunities for participation
- Uses positive presuppositions when responding to and inquiring of others

Pursuing a Balance Between Advocacy and Inquiry
- Advocates for own ideas and inquires into the ideas of others
- Acts to provide equitable opportunities for participation
- Presents rationale for positions, including assumptions, facts, and feelings
- Disagrees respectfully and openly with ideas and offers rationale for disagreement
- Inquires of others about their reasons for reaching and occupying a position

Reprinted from Garmston & Wellman (1999) with permission of Christopher-Gordon Publishers.

FIGURE 6.10
Assessing the Seven Norms of Collaborative Work

	Low				High
Pausing	•	•	•	•	•
Paraphrasing	•	•	•	•	•
Probing	•	•	•	•	•
Putting Ideas on the Table	•	•	•	•	•
Paying Attention to Self and Others	•	•	•	•	•
Presuming Positive Intentions	•	•	•	•	•
Pursuing Advocacy or Inquiry	•	•	•	•	•

Reprinted from Garmston & Wellman (1999) with permission of Christopher-Gordon Publishers.

Communicate your results. The results of your data analysis must be shared—the disappointing with the exhilarating. These results form the foundation for your next efforts in impact-focused inquiry, and probing results is an essential collaborative norm. Share your results with your colleagues in an open forum. Ask them to communicate their responses, individually and collectively, through drawing, mapping, and writing. Discuss key words in phrases in the results, how they are used, and what they mean. Suspend discussion of solutions for a time—let the results incubate, and then return to them in a focused planning session.

THE FOUR SHIPS

The shared journey is nurtured through its grounding in a collaborative learning environment. As illustrated in Figure 6.11, Carol Moffatt (2002) and Vince Ham (2002) have identified the four ships of collaboration.

Ownership

How do leaders build ownership? This step requires that the vision be clear and communicated so that all can identify its themes, even though all

FIGURE 6.11

The Four Ships of Collaboration

Adapted and derived from work by Ham (2002) and from Moffatt (2002).

may not agree. Leaders must be personally active in ensuring that the agenda does not stray from this vision and that they are not alone in supporting the actions and the time allotment. Developing and nurturing a shared perspective, with continual opportunities for all to share in shaping that perspective, must be a major organizational priority. Perhaps most important, the vision must not overspecify details of implementation: ownership results when participants have broad opportunity to define their work within clear expectations for contributing results that further the vision.

Leadership

In a collaborative learning environment, leaders support collaboration by providing resources, offering feedback, and setting performance expectations. They model collaboration as they devote their energy, time, and expertise to the collaborative process. Leaders create opportunities for collaboration and are judicious about when to participate actively and when to stay away. They provide opportunities for collaborators to communicate successes throughout the organization and they recognize and reward these successes. Leaders are accessible, responsive, and generous in promoting shared leadership.

Relationship

Collaboration is hard work, normally above and beyond the requirements of the job. Why, then, do people bother to collaborate? Eventually it may be because they recognize that collaboration is a superior way to support the vision. But commitment to collaboration almost always begins in relationships. Leaders recognize this truth and look for opportunities to broker new working relationships. Everyone is encouraged to participate and contribute, and they are given multiple avenues for doing so. Leaders actively recognize the contributions of all individuals while emphasizing the power of the group. In a collaborative working environment, more and more people will take time to recognize and reward the contributions of their colleagues.

Fellowship

One definition of fellowship (American Heritage Dictionary, 2000) is *the companionship of individuals in a congenial atmosphere and on equal terms*. By building ownership for a clear vision; setting collaborative leadership as a high priority; building relationships through focused, challenging work; and sharing and celebrating individual contributions and collaborative successes, it is possible to build a foundation of fellowship throughout the organization.

These four ships carry us on the shared journey. Each is essential to our success in building a positive and productive collaborative learning environment for all educators; together they represent the challenges and opportunities for leaders in building a collaborative organization, sustaining learning communities, and creating dynamic schools.

APPENDIX

MONTHLY FOCUS CHART
FOR MENTORING

AUGUST Mentor

Logistics	Possible Questions for Your Mentee
• Set appointments to meet for the first three months. • Set ground rules for communicating and relating.	• What questions do these resources pose to you? • What do you need? • How can I help you? • About what do you feel most concerned?

AUGUST Mentee

Informational	Instructional	Personal
Do you know the policies and procedures of the school and district? Do you have district emergency phone numbers? Do you know who's who? You need a staff list with grade level and department members and key resource people (including team leader, department chair, mentor, office manager, aides, secretaries, counselors, and custodians) Do you have a map of the school? Are you familiar with the physical setup of the school and location of key facilities? (staff restrooms, staff phones, AV areas, professional library, copy machines, and staff lounge) Have you reviewed the faculty handbook, student handbook, school calendar, and the policies and procedures manual? Are you familiar with lunch procedures? Do you understand class and teacher schedules, and extra duty responsibilities? How are parents involved with the school (e.g., volunteers, parent clubs, local school advisory committee)?	Is the classroom organized for learning? Have you acquired course guides, curriculum guides, class outlines, and goal statements for subjects assigned? Do you have necessary supplies to begin the year (including tape, staples, and construction paper)? Have you sketched curriculum plans for the first month? Have you planned the first week in detail? Has your mentor critiqued the plan for your first week?	Do you have a calendar that has spaces for appointments from when you get up until you go to sleep? Does it include space for the weekend, too? (time management)

AUGUST Mentee (continued)

Management	Results	Collaboration
What is your process for establishing the behavior rules for the classroom? What are the behavior rules in your classroom?		Have you set a meeting schedule with your mentor for the first three months of school?
Are you acquainted with the discipline procedures and policies of the school?		Which of the following will you do this month?
Do you have the referral procedure for the educational support team (EST)?		Observe a colleague. Share teacher resource materials. Attend a workshop with a colleague.
Do you have copies of necessary forms, such as referral, attendance, and hall passes?		Participate in a study group session.
Do the student policies make sense to you? Have you asked your mentor for clarification, if needed?		Videotape a lesson and critique it. Exchange an article from a professional journal.
Are you satisfied with the procedures for classroom routines? (passing out materials, taking attendance, and collecting assignments)?		Meet for a breakfast discussion. Read and discuss a professional book.
Is your classroom set up? (Are desks, tables, supply area, assignment baskets, and bulletin boards organized?)		Review student work with your mentor.
Are you happy with your chosen lesson plan format? Does it work for you? What needs to change?		Other: _____
Are you satisfied with the grade book? What will be your system for keeping track of assessment information?		
Do you have a system for keeping track of parent contacts and discipline referrals?		

SEPTEMBER Mentor

Logistics	Possible Questions for Your Mentee
• How do you monitor and adjust your operating style to the mentee's in order to build the relationship?	• What is the biggest issue facing you? • Where are you with these tasks? • What problems have you encountered? • How are you taking care of yourself?

SEPTEMBER Mentee

Informational	Instructional	Personal
Have you read your school's action plan? Are you responsible for any action steps? Is there anything that you do not understand? Have you asked your mentor to explain any aspects of the action plan that are confusing?	Do you have long-range general plans for the first quarter? (e.g., units, time lines, materials ordered) Are you modeling what you expect from students? Have you read your students' IEPs? What are the implications for you? What questions do you have? How might you get these answered?	How are you using time? Who could help you with some tasks? What is working well for you?

Management	Results	Collaboration
Are you reinforcing expectations? How is the implementation of rules, procedures, and management systems going? Are you grading, recording, and returning those tasks that you feel are important for feedback as soon as possible?	Are there assessments from the school action plan for which you are responsible? Are you familiar with state assessments, portfolios, and local assessments? Have you put assessment dates on your calendar? What additional assessments do you need? Are you beginning to save samples of student work to use as possible benchmarks? Are you familiar with the district's teacher evaluation document?	Do you have two dates scheduled to meet with your mentor?

OCTOBER Mentor

Possible Questions for Your Mentee:

- What is the biggest issue facing you?
- Where are you with these tasks?
- What problems have you encountered?
- How are you taking care of yourself?

OCTOBER Mentee

Informational	Instructional	Personal
What statewide professional development activities are available? What contract obligations pertain to you?	What are the instructional issues that are most difficult for you? Are you familiar with your school's supervision and evaluation process? Have you discussed these with your principal?	Are you meeting your goals?

Management	Results	Collaboration
		Are you familiar with parent and teacher conferencing procedures and techniques? Have you tried using e-mail to check in with your mentor?

NOVEMBER Mentor

Logistics	Possible Questions for Your Mentee
• Have you set time to meet with your mentee for the next three months?	• What is the biggest issue facing you? • Where are you with these tasks? • What problems have you encountered? • How are you taking care of yourself?

NOVEMBER Mentee

Informational	Instructional	Personal
	Are you setting up a demonstration lesson and making time for debriefing with your mentor? What new instructional strategies might you try this month?	How are you taking care of yourself? Do you know what health and wellness supports are offered in your school or outside your school?

Management	Results	Collaboration
Are the behaviors of any students challenging for you? What might you do? Is there a need to make referrals to the educational support team?		Have you set dates for meetings with your mentor for the next three months? Have you considered membership in any professional organizations?

DECEMBER Mentor

Logistics	Possible Questions for Your Mentee:
• Have you met on your scheduled meeting date?	• What is the biggest issue facing you? • Where are you with these tasks? • What problems have you encountered? Is there one that we might work on solving together? • How are you taking care of yourself?

DECEMBER Mentee

Informational	Instructional	Personal
		Are you getting done what you need and want to get done? Have you checked your priorities list to see if what you are doing is meeting your priority areas? Are you regularly using your calendar? What are you doing for winter break?

Management	Results	Collaboration
Have you kept up needed contact with parents?	Are you developing and using classroom assessments? Do you have an assessment plan for units of study?	Do you have two meetings scheduled with your mentor? Have you set a time to observe your mentor in the classroom and to debrief?

JANUARY Mentor

Logistics	Possible Questions for Your Mentee
• Are you meeting with your mentee at the scheduled meeting time? • Have you set meeting times for the next three months?	• What have been the high points of this semester? • What have you learned? • What do you hope to change?

JANUARY Mentee

Informational	Instructional	Personal

Management	Results	Collaboration
What are your long-range plans for second semester?	Have you begun preparing for the next reporting period? What assessments do you have? What do you need?	Are you meeting with your mentor at the scheduled meeting time? Have you reflected on the first semester together?

FEBRUARY Mentor

Logistics	Possible Questions for Your Mentee
• Are you meeting with your mentee on your scheduled meeting date?	• What is the biggest issue facing you? • Where are you with these tasks? • What problems have you encountered? • How are you taking care of yourself?

FEBRUARY Mentee

Informational	Instructional	Personal
Are you familiar with resources available from federal programs, including Title I and II?	Are you preparing students for state and local assessments in late March or early April, if applicable? Are you giving practice tests and using benchmarks for discussion?	

Management	Results	Collaboration
		Are you meeting with your mentor at the scheduled meeting time? Which of the following activities will you do this month (or substitute something similar)? Observe a colleague. Share teacher resource materials. Attend a workshop with a colleague. Participate in a study group session. Videotape a lesson and critique it. Exchange an article from a professional journal. Meet for a breakfast discussion. Read and discuss a professional book. Review student work with your mentor. Other: _____

MARCH Mentor

Logistics	Possible Questions for Your Mentee
• Are you meeting your mentee at the scheduled time?	• What is the biggest issue facing you? • Where are you with these tasks? • What problems have you encountered? • How are you taking care of yourself?

MARCH Mentee

Informational	Instructional	Personal
Review school policy and procedures for student promotion.		

Management	Results	Collaboration
Have you organized your lesson plans and schedule to accommodate state and local assessments if appropriate? Are you continuing to connect with parents?		Are you meeting with your mentor at the scheduled time? Which of the following will you do this month? Observe a colleague. Share teacher resource materials. Attend a workshop with a colleague. Participate in a study group session. Videotape a lesson and critique it. Exchange an article from a professional journal. Meet for a breakfast discussion. Read and discuss a professional book. Review student work with your mentor. Other: _____

APRIL Mentor

Logistics	Possible Questions for Your Mentee
• Are you meeting at the scheduled meeting time with your mentee?	• What is the biggest issue facing you? • Where are you with these tasks? • What problems have you encountered? • How are you taking care of yourself?

APRIL Mentee

Informational	Instructional	Personal
		Are you meeting your priority areas? Are you setting time aside for exercise, relaxation, family, and friends?

Management	Results	Collaboration

		Are you meeting with your mentor at the scheduled time?
		Which of the following will you do this month?
		    Observe a colleague.
		    Share teacher resource materials.
		    Attend a workshop with a colleague.
		    Participate in a study group session.
		    Videotape a lesson and critique it.
		    Exchange an article from a professional journal.
		    Meet for a breakfast discussion.
		    Read and discuss a professional book.
		    Review student work with your mentor.
		    Other: _____

MAY Mentor

Logistics	Possible Questions for Your Mentee
• Are you meeting with your mentee at the scheduled time?	• Where are you with these tasks? • What problems have you encountered? • How are you taking care of yourself?

MAY Mentee

Informational	Instructional	Personal
Do you know the school and district policies regarding special end-of-year activities, assemblies, and parties?	Have you sketched your curriculum plan for the next six weeks? Can you write, in detail, your curriculum plan for the last week of school? Have you asked your mentor to critique it?	

Management	Results	Collaboration
		Plan for summer coursework or workshops.

JUNE Mentor

- Have you set up a time with your mentee to share how the year went for both of you?

- How will you give closure to your time together?

JUNE Mentee

Informational	Instructional	Personal
What are the processes and procedures necessary for closing school?		How will you celebrate the successful end of your first year? About what accomplishments do you feel proud? What do you most want to change next year?

Management	Results	Collaboration
Have you recorded end-of-year grades in student portfolios and records? Have you completed report cards? Have you returned books and keys, and stored materials and equipment?		Have you set up a time to meet with your mentor?

REFERENCES AND RESOURCES

Acheson, K. A., & Gall, M. D. (1997). *Techniques in the clinical supervision of teachers* (4th ed.). White Plains, NY: Longman.

The American heritage dictionary of the English language. (2000). Boston: Houghton-Mifflin.

Appleby, J. (1998). *Becoming critical friends: Reflections of a NSRF coach.* Providence, RI: Annenberg Institute for School Reform at Brown University.

Baker, R. G., & Showers, B. (1984). *The effects of a coaching strategy on teachers' transfer of training to classroom practice: A six-month follow-up study.* Paper presented at the annual meeting of the American Education Research Association, New Orleans, LA.

Bates, P., & Wilson, T. (1989). *Critical issues in the education of black children.* Ann Arbor, MI: University of Michigan.

Blythe, Y., Allen, D., & Powell, B. S. (1999). *Looking together at student work: A companion guide to assessing student learning.* New York: Teachers College Press.

Braddock, C. (1997). *Body voices.* Berkeley, CA: Page Mill Press.

Brewer, K. C. (1988). *Getting things done: An achiever's guide to time management.* Shawnee Mission, KS: National Press Publications.

Calhoun, E. (1993). Action research: Three approaches. *Educational Leadership, 51*(2), 62–65.

Calkins, L. M. (1994). The art of teaching writing. Portsmouth, NH: Heinemann.

Carr, J., & Harris, D. (1993). *Getting it together: A process workbook for K–12 curriculum development, implementation, and assessment.* Needham Heights, MA: Allyn & Bacon.

Carr, J. F., & Harris, D. E. (2001). *Succeeding with standards: Linking curriculum, assessment, and action planning.* Alexandria, VA: ASCD.

Center for Cognitive Coaching. (2000). [Web site]. www.cognitivecoaching.com.

Coalition of Essential Schools. (2002). How we are different [Web page]. Available: http://www.essentialschools.org/pub/ces_docs/about/phil/how_different.html

Costa, A. L., & Garmston, R. J. (2002). *Cognitive Coaching. A foundation for renaissance schools.* Norwood, MA: Christopher-Gordon.

Covey, S. R. (1990). *The seven habits of highly effective people.* New York: Simon & Schuster.

DeBolt, G. (1989). [Report]. Helpful elements in mentoring of first year teachers. Report given to State Education Department on New York State Mentor Teacher-Internship Program for 1988–1989.

DuFour, R. (2002, May). The learning-centered principal. *Educational Leadership, 59*(8),12–18.

DuFour, R., Eaker, R. E., & Baker, R. (1998). *Professional learning communities at work: Best practices for enhancing student achievement.* Bloomington, IN: National Educational Service.

Dunne, F., Nave, B., & Lewis, A. (2000). Critical friends groups: Teachers helping teachers to improve student learning. *The Research Bulletin* (No. 28). Bloomington, IN: Center for Evaluation, Development and Research.

Educational Testing Service. (1999). *PATHWISE framework induction program.* Princeton, NJ: Author.

Elmore, R. (2002). Hard questions about practice. *Educational Leadership, 59*(8), 22–25.

Fritz, R. (1999). *The path of least resistance for managers.* San Francisco: Barrett-Koehler.

Froese, E. E. (2002). Professional growth programs. In Wideen, M., *The professional development dissortium.* Port of Spain: Ministry of Education of Trinidad and Tobago.

Fullan, M. (2001). *Leading in a culture of change.* San Francisco, CA: Jossey-Bass.

Fullan, M. (2002, December). *Leading in a culture of change.* Paper presented at the meeting of the National Staff Development Association, Boston, MA.

Garmston, R. (1987, February). How administrators support peer coaching. *Educational Leadership, 44*(5), 18–26.

Garmston, R., & Wellman, B. (1999). *The adaptive school: Developing and facilitating collaborative groups.* Norwood, MA: Christopher-Gordon.

Gless, J., & Baron, W. (1996). *A guide to prepare support providers for work with beginning teachers.* [Training module]. Santa Cruz, CA: Santa Cruz County Office of Education, 24–26.

Glickman, C. D. (2002). *Leadership for learning: How to help teachers succeed.* Athens, GA: Institute for Schools, Education, and Democracy.

Glickman, C. (1990). *Supervision of instruction: A developmental approach* (2nd ed.). Boston: Allyn and Bacon.

Glickman, C. (1997). *Supervision of instruction: A developmental approach* (4th ed.). Boston: Allyn and Bacon.

Goleman, D. (2000). *Working with emotional intelligence.* New York: Bantam.

Gordon, S. P. (1991). *How to help beginning teachers succeed.* Alexandria, VA: Association for Supervision and Curriculum Development.

Graham, B. L., & Fahey, K. (1999). School leaders look at student work. *Educational Leadership, 66*(6), 25–27.

Ham, V. (2002, April). What teachers and students use computers for in New Zealand classrooms: Results from the IC TPD cluster schools research project. [Paper]. Presented to the Infovision Innovations Stream conference. Christchurch: NZ.

Harris, D., Brandenburg, R., & Gibson, D. (2002). *The Vermont Institutes: A white paper.* Montpelier, VT: The Vermont Institutes.

Harvey, S. (1998). *Nonfiction matters: Reading, writing, and research in grades 3–8.* Portland, ME: Stenhouse.

Harvey, S., & Goudvis, A. (2000). *Strategies that work: Teaching comprehension to enhance understanding.* Portland, ME: Stenhouse.

Hesselbein, F. (2002). *Leader to leader.* San Francisco: Jossey-Bass.

Hochheiser, R. M. (1992). *Time management.* New York: Barrons.

Huling-Austin, L., & Murphy, S. C. (1987). *Assessing the impact of teacher induction programs: Implications for program development.* Austin, TX: Texas University. (ERIC Document Reproduction Service No. ED 283 779)

Johnson, D.W., & Johnson, R.T. (1994). Learning together. In Sharan, S., *Handbook of cooperative learning methods* (pp. 51–65). Westport, CT: Greenwood Press.

Joyce, B., & Calhoun, E. (1998). *Learning to teach productively.* Needham Heights, MA: Allyn and Bacon.

Joyce, B. R., & Showers, B. (1987). Low cost arrangements for peer coaching. *The Journal of Staff Development, 8*(1), 22–24.

Joyce, B., & Showers, B. (1983). *Power in staff development through research on training.* Alexandria, VA: Association for Supervision and Curriculum Development.

Joyce, B., & Weil, M. (1996). *Models of teaching* (5th ed.). Boston: Allyn & Bacon.

Kruse, S., Seashore-Louis, K., & Byrk, A. (1994). *Building professional community in schools.* Madison, WI: Center on Organization and Restructuring of Schools, University of Wisconsin.

Leggett, D., & Hoyle, S. (1987). Peer coaching: One district's experience in using teachers as staff developers. *Journal of Staff Development, 8*(1), 16–19.

Lewis, A. (1998, March/April). Teachers in the driver's seat: Collaborative assessment proves a positive way to reform schools and improve teaching. *Harvard Education Letter: Research Online.* http://www.edletter.org/past/issues/1998-ma/teacher.shtml

Love, N. (2002). *Using data/getting results: A practical guide for school improvement in math and science.* Norwood, MA: Christopher-Gordon.

Martin, D. (2002). Linkage model of educational development for Trinidad and Tobago. In Wideen, M. *The professional development dissortium.* Port of Spain: Ministry of Education of Trinidad and Tobago.

Martin, H., & Martin, C. (1989). *Martin operating styles inventory.* San Diego, CA: Organization Improvement Systems. Available: http://www.ois-martin.com.

Marzano, R. (1992). *A different kind of classroom.* Alexandria, VA: ASCD.

Mellette, S., & McCollum, K. (2005). World class excellence in Richland Two: The foundations of a mentoring program. Columbia, SC: Richland Two School District. Unpublished.

Moffatt, C. (2002, Oct. 12). Presentation to ASCD Executive Council, Wellington, New Zealand.

Mohr, N., & Dichter, A. (n.d.). *Stages of team development: Lessons from the struggles of site-based management.* Providence, RI: Annenberg Institute for School Reform at Brown University. Available: http://www.annenberginstitute.org/images/Stages.pdf

Murphy, C. (1991). Lessons from a journey into change. *Educational Leadership, 48*(8), 63–67.

Murphy, C. (1999, Spring). Using time for faculty study. *The Journal of Staff Development, 18*(3), 20–24.

Murphy, C., & Lick, D. C. (1998). *Whole faculty study groups: A powerful way to change schools and enhance student learning.* Thousand Oaks, CA: Corwin.

National School Reform Faculty. (n.d.). *Critical friends groups as a vehicle for improving student learning.* Bloomington, IN: Harmony School Education Center.

National Systemic Improvement Initiative. (2001). *Systemic improvement protocol.* Hartford, CT: The Connecticut Academy.

Odell, S. J., & Ferraro, D. P. (1992). Teacher mentoring and teacher retention. *Journal of Teacher Education, 43*(3), 200.

Payne, R. (2001). *Framework for understanding poverty.* Highlands, TX: aha! Process.

Pinnell, G., & Scharer, P. (Eds.). (2001). *Extending our reach: Teaching for comprehension in reading, grades K–2.* Columbus, OH: The Literacy Collaborative at The Ohio State University.

Podsen, I., & Denmark, V. (2000). *Coaching and mentoring first-year and student teachers.* Larchmont, NY: Eye On Education.

Robbins, P. (1991). *How to plan and implement a peer coaching program.* Alexandria, VA: Association for Supervision and Curriculum Development.

Routman, R. (2000). *Conversations.* Portsmouth, NH: Heinemann.

Sagor, R. D. (1992). *How to conduct collaborative action research.* Alexandria, VA: Association for Supervision and Curriculum Development.

Saphier, J., & Gower, R. (1997). *The skillful teacher: Building your teaching skills* (5th ed.). Acton, MA: Research for Better Teaching.

Scholtes, P. R. (1992). *The team handbook: How to use teams to improve quality.* Madison, WI: Joiner.

Seidel, S., Walters, J., Kirby, E., Olff, N., Powell, K., Scripp, L., & Veenema, S. (1997). *Portfolio practices: Thinking through the assessment of children's work.* Washington, DC: National Education Association Publishing Library.

Sergiovanni, T., & Starratt, R. (1997). *Supervision: A redefinition.* Columbus, OH: McGraw-Hill.

Showers, B., & Joyce, B. (1996). The evolution of peer coaching. *Educational Leadership, 53*(6), 12–16.

Sparks, D. (1990, Spring). Cognitive coaching: An interview with Robert Garmston. *Journal of Staff Development, 11*(2), 12–15.

Sparks, D. (1998, Fall). Interview with Bruce Joyce: Making assessment part of teacher learning. *Journal of Staff Development, 19*(4), 33–35.

Stiggins, R., & Knight, T. (1997). *But are they learning?: A commonsense parents' guide to assessment and grading in school.* Portland, OR: Assessment Training Institute.

Thompson-Grove, G. (2001). *Creating professional communities to improve student learning.* Presentation at the Vermont Standards and Assessment Consortium meeting, Montpelier, VT.

Tuckman, B. (1965). Developmental sequence in small groups. *Psychological Bulletin, 63* (384–389).

Vermont Department of Education. (1998). *Standards into action: Professional development toolkit for standards-based education.* Montpelier, VT: Vermont Department of Education.

Vermont Department of Education. (1999). *Using standards in the classroom: A teacher resource guide.* Montpelier, VT: Author.

Wolfe, P., & Robbins, P. (program consultants). (1989). *Opening doors: An introduction to peer coaching* [Videotape]. Alexandria, VA: Association for Supervision and Curriculum Development.

INDEX

Page numbers followed by an *f* refer to a figure.

About the Authors

Judy F. Carr is associate professor in the Educational Leadership Department at the University of South Florida, Sarasota/Manatee. She is co-editor of *Integrated Studies in the Middle Grades: Dancing Through Walls* (Teachers College Press, 1993) and co-editor of *Living and Learning in the Middle Grades: The Dance Continues: A Festschrift for Chris Stevenson* (National Middle School Association, 2001).

Nancy Herman has recently retired from her work as an independent consultant specializing in mentor training, literacy development, and middle grades education. She is a certified yoga instructor and massage therapist who conducts classes and retreats for educators and others at So Just Relax in Shelburne, Vermont (www.sojustrelax.com).

Douglas E. Harris is executive director of the Vermont Institutes, an organization dedicated to supporting collaborative reform efforts at all levels of education—classroom, local, and state. He has been a teacher, assistant superintendent, and superintendent of schools.

Carr and Harris are co-authors of *Succeeding with Standards: Linking Curriculum, Assessment, and Action Planning* (ASCD, 2001), *How to Use Standards in the Classroom* (ASCD, 1996), and *Getting It Together: A Process Workbook for K–12 Curriculum Development, Implementation and Assessment* (Allyn & Bacon, 1993).

Carr and Harris are consultants with the Center for Curriculum Renewal (www.curriculum renewal.com), offering coaching, facilitation, program development, and program evaluation services and workshops to schools and districts, state departments of education, and other educational organizations. They can be reached at 802-598-8292 or CCRlearn@aol.com.

Related ASCD Resources

Creating Dynamic Schools Through Mentoring, Coaching, and Collaboration

At the time of publication, the following ASCD resources were available; for the most up-to-date information about ASCD resources, go to www.ascd.org. ASCD stock numbers are noted in parentheses.

Audio

Beyond Induction: Become Passionate About Improving Professional Practice by Audrey Lakin (Audiotape # 203211; CD #503304)

Bold Leadership: The Rocky Path to Excellence by Pam Robbins and Harvey Alvy (Audiotape #202160)

Developing Mentoring Programs for Professional Excellence by Pam Robbins (Audiotape #203082)

Leading and Building Community in the Swampy Lowlands of No Easy Answers by Robert Bastress, Betty Collins, Gail Covington McBride, and Eric Mills (CD # 504310)

Multimedia

Educational Leadership on CD-ROM, 1992-98 (#598223)

Creating the Capacity for Change by Jody Mason Westbrook and Valarie Spiser-Albert (#702118)

Guide for Instructional Leaders, Guide 1: An ASCD Action Tool by Roland Barth, Bobb Darnell, Laura Lipton, and Bruce Wellman (#702110)

Books

The Art of School Leadership by Thomas R. Hoerr (#105037)

Promises Kept: Sustaining School and District Leadership in a Turbulent Era by Steven Jay Gross (#101078)

School Leadership That Works: From Research to Results by Robert J. Marzano, Timothy Waters, and Brian A. McNulty (#105125)

The Hero's Journey: How Educators Can Transform Schools and Improve Learning by John L. Brown and Cerylle A. Moffett (#199002)

Lessons from Exceptional School Leaders by Mark F. Goldberg (#101229)

1997 ASCD Yearbook: Rethinking Educational Change with Heart and Mind edited by Andy Hargreaves (#197000)

Staying Centered: Curriculum Leadership In a Turbulent Era by Steven Jay Gross (#198008)

Networks

Visit the ASCD Web site (www.ascd.org) and search for "networks" for information about professional educators who have formed groups in the categories of "Instructional Supervision" and "Performance Assessment for Leadership." Look in the "Network Directory" for current facilitators' addresses and phone numbers.

For more information, visit us on the World Wide Web (http://www.ascd.org), send an e-mail message to member@ascd.org, call the ASCD Service Center (1-800-933-ASCD or 703-578-9600, then press 2), send a fax to 703-575-5400, or write to Information Services, ASCD, 1703 N. Beauregard St., Alexandria, VA 22311-1714 USA.